Hulton BEC books:

NUMERACY AND ACCOUNTING

National Award

Other Hulton BEC Books:

for BEC General

People and Communication   0 7175 0832 3

The World of Work   0 7175 0833 1

Business Calculations   0 7175 0834 X

for BEC National

The Organisation in its Environment—Part One   0 7175 0836 6

The Organisation in its Environment—Part Two   0 7175 0837 4

Business Administration   0 7175 0838 2

Business Law   0 7175 0839 0

Secretarial Services   0 7175 0840 4

The Organisation and Economics of Distribution   0 7175 0842 0

People and Communication   0 7175 0843 9

Other Hulton books:

Principles of Accounts   0 7175 0683 5

NUMERACY AND ACCOUNTING

Gill Wilkinson, B.A., A.C.A.
Lecturer in Accounting
Windsor and Maidenhead College

Advisory Editor: Patricia Callender, B.Sc.(Econ.)
Head of Department of Business Studies
Windsor and Maidenhead College

HULTON EDUCATIONAL PUBLICATIONS

© 1981   Gill Wilkinson

ISBN 0 7175 0841 2

First published 1981 by
Hulton Educational Publications Ltd.,
Raans Road, Amersham, Bucks. HP6 6JJ

Photoset by Computacomp (UK) Ltd.
Printed and bound in Great Britain by
Richard Clay (The Chaucer Press) Ltd., Bungay.

Preface

This book covers the syllabus for Module 2 of the BEC National Award, Numeracy and Accounting.

Each chapter falls into a standard pattern of definition – where appropriate, explanation, technical matters and book-keeping, with copious examples. This is followed by a summary for quick revision and a number of questions. Answers have not been given as, in most cases, the exercise lies in the correct presentation of the material, rather than in the numerical calculation. The ability to find the correct Net Profit, and then to see this as the 'answer' can give a student a sense of false confidence. The exception is in Chapter 2, where both answers and explanations have been given, on account of the purely mathematical and logical nature of the questions.

It is intended that the book should be sufficiently comprehensive and self-explanatory for a student to work through a chapter alone if necessary. This is a useful feature, as absenteeism is a major hazard on day-release courses.

The first two chapters deal with arithmetic. Theoretically a student will have already obtained this information during his schooldays. However, for those who have temporarily mislaid the facts in the labyrinth of their memories, the chapters cover the fundamental principles, and show several short-cuts for mental calculations. This is necessary when calculators may not be used in examinations. Chapter 3 includes details of the basic accounting concepts and conventions, an understanding of which is essential for the modern manager. Basic book-keeping is covered in Chapters 4 to 17, and these are designed to be worked through consecutively as each builds on information and skills previously acquired. Chapter 11 on the subsidiary books deals with the recording of VAT and the documentation required by the Customs and Excise, which is a necessary and practical exercise. The chapters on statistics may be worked in any order, and could be interspersed with the book-keeping to give a little light relief.

Finally I would like to thank the publishers and my many friends who contributed to this book for all their help and advice. I also wish to acknowledge Michael, Marie and my long-suffering husband without whom this book would never have been written.

Contents

Chapter 1 ARITHMETIC 1 Arithmetical calculations, fractions, decimals, ratios and percentages

1 The Digits

Numbers are composed of digits. A digit is an individual numeral: there are ten of them—0, 1, 2, 3, 4, 5, 6, 7, 8, 9. The value placed on a digit depends on its position in the number:

```
H T U
1 0 0
  1 0
    1
-------
1 1 1
```

So the first 1 is one hundred, the second 1 is ten and the third 1 is one unit. The correct positioning of these figures is vital, as there is a considerable difference between $1 + 1 = 2$ and $1 + 10 = 11$.

2 Addition

Accurate addition is important. It is most helpful if figures are listed in vertical columns so that the hundreds, tens and units are directly below one another. To avoid errors in carrying figures from one column to another and to help in checking the addition, the figure to be carried can be written below in pencil.

```
 9,540
 7,631
 4,279
 3,467
24,917
 1 21
```

When adding a substantial column of figures in the office, a calculator or adding machine will probably be used. It is easy to make a mistake when entering a figure on a machine, and therefore important to know the approximate answer. This can quickly be found if the figures are rounded. Using the above example:

	Rounded
9,540	10,000
7,631	8,000
4,279	4,000
3,467	3,000
24,917	25,000

The actual answer, 24,917, is close to the approximate answer of 25,000 and so may be presumed to be correct. Rounding can easily be done mentally and is useful when checking addition in examinations.

Another method of checking addition is known as cross-casting. This is a combination of vertical and horizontal addition. For example:

Accounts department time sheets

	Monday		Tuesday		Wednesday		Thursday		Friday		Total
J. Bloggs	8	+	8	+	8	+	8	+	9	=	41
K. Dodd	9	+	8	+	$8\frac{1}{2}$	+	$7\frac{1}{2}$	+	10	=	43
G. Greene	8	+	9	+	$10\frac{1}{2}$	+	9	+	$8\frac{1}{2}$	=	45
H. Hall	8	+	8	+	9	+	8	+	8	=	41
S. Mudd	8	+	9	+	9	+	9	+	9	=	44
	41	+	42	+	45	+	$41\frac{1}{2}$	+	$44\frac{1}{2}$	=	214

The total column on the right shows the individual's total hours for the week. Joe Bloggs worked for 41 hours that week. The total column at the bottom shows the hours worked on a particular day, so 41 hours were worked on Monday. The figure in the bottom right hand corner represents the total hours worked during the week. It is the sum of the individual worker's hours, and also the sum of the daily totals. If the two figures do not agree a mistake has been made and the addition must be checked. These figures are usually set out without the plus and equals signs.

This format is used in cash books and day books and is dealt with in the accounting chapters.

3 Subtraction

Subtraction is the opposite of addition; however, many people find addition easier and more mistakes are made in subtraction. For this reason change in shops is usually given by the addition method. For example, if a £5 note is given for an article costing £3·50, change would be given of 50 pence to make the sum up to £4, and of £1 to make the sum up to £5.

This is relatively easy when dealing with real money, but the same principle can be applied to theoretical subtraction. For example:

Subtract 64 from 132:

First round up the smaller figure to 100 by adding 36.
Then add 36 to the larger number $132 + 36 = 168$.
The answer to the new sum is easily found $168 - 100 = 68$.

With four-figure numbers the lower number is rounded to the nearest thousand. For example:

Subtract 5,673 from 8,764:

Round up the smaller figure to 6,000 by adding 327.
Then add 327 to 8,764 giving 9,091.
The new sum becomes $9,091 - 6,000 = 3,091$.

Sometimes one is given a column of figures some of which are to be added, positive numbers, and some of which are to be subtracted, negative numbers. When this happens the figures to be subtracted are shown in brackets. For example, the calculation $26 + 34 + 15 - 45 + 37 = 67$ would appear as:

$$
\begin{array}{r}
26 \\
34 \\
15 \\
(45) \\
\underline{37} \\
\underline{67}
\end{array}
$$

This combination of addition and subtraction is known as casting.

4 Multiplication

The key to fast and accurate multiplication is a sound knowledge of the tables. Fortunately, it is rarely necessary to perform complicated long multiplication as there are several shortcuts. However, practice is required in selecting the most suitable method for solving the problem.

(a) MULTIPLICATION BY DIVISION

This can be done if the multiplier bears a suitable relationship to 10.
For example: 192×5
This can be done using the five times table, or more quickly by dividing by 2 and then multiplying by 10 as 5 is half of 10.
$192 \div 2 = 96$. To multiply by ten simply add a nought and the answer is 960.
If the multiplier was 50, one would divide by 2 and add two noughts; if 500, divide by 2 and add 3 noughts.
$2\frac{1}{2}$ is a quarter of 10, so when multiplying by $2\frac{1}{2}$ it is possible to divide by 4 and

add a nought. For example: $192 \times 2\frac{1}{2}$

First divide by 4, giving the answer 48.
Then add a nought giving a product of 480.

The same principle applies to 25 and 250.
$7\frac{1}{2}$ is three quarters of 10, so when multiplying by it one can divide by 4, multiply by 3 and add a nought.
This may sound complicated but in practice it is extremely simple. For example: $192 \times 7\frac{1}{2}$

First divide by 4 giving 48, then multiply by 3 to give 144, finally add a nought to find the product of 1,440.

This can be used for 75, 750, 7,500 and so forth.

(b) MULTIPLICATION BY SUBTRACTION

If the multiplier ends in a nine it can be rounded up to the number following.
For example: 9×76

$$
\begin{array}{lr}
10 \times 76 & = 760 \\
\text{Then subtract the additional} & (76) \\
\text{To give the answer} & \overline{684}
\end{array}
$$

The same principle applies to more complicated examples, for instance: 854×99

$$
\begin{array}{lr}
854 \times 100 & = 85{,}400 \\
\text{Then subtract the additional} & (854) \\
& \overline{84{,}546}
\end{array}
$$

A similar calculation can be performed if the multiplier is just over a ten.
For example: 11×76

$$
\begin{array}{lr}
10 \times 76 = 760 \\
\text{Then add an additional} & 76 \\
& \overline{836}
\end{array}
$$

Methods can be combined, for example: 348×15

$$
\begin{array}{lr}
\text{First multiply by 10} & 348 \times 10 = 3{,}480 \\
\text{Then divide the answer by 2} & 1{,}740 \\
& \overline{5{,}220}
\end{array}
$$

The last two examples are just variations on standard long multiplication.

(c) MULTIPLICATION BY FACTORS

A factor of a number is one which will divide into it exactly. For example 12 and 4

13

are factors of 48. These factors can be subdivided, $4 = 2 \times 2$, and $12 = 2 \times 2 \times 3$. So 48 can be expressed as

$$2 \times 2 \times 2 \times 2 \times 3 \text{ or as } 2^4 \times 3$$

To use this method one would concentrate on the larger factors of 12 and 4. In order to multiply 479 by 48:

First calculate: $479 \times 4 = 1,916$

Then multiply the product by 12:
$1,916 \times 12 = 22,992$.

So $479 \times 48 = 22,992$.

In practice this method is only suitable for small multipliers which factorise easily.

(d) STANDARD LONG MULTIPLICATION

Methods (a) to (c) are only suitable in certain circumstances, although they will be found to have a wide range of applications. Goods are sold in metric quantities, which usually give convenient numbers for multiplication such as 250, 500 and 750.

There is little point in spending half an hour deciding on the most appropriate short cut when the multiplication will only take two minutes. Because long multiplication involves moving the decimal point it is essential that it is set out correctly. For example: 587×333

$$
\begin{array}{r}
587 \times 333 \\
\times\,333 \\
\hline
176,100 \\
17,610 \\
1,761 \\
\hline
195,471 \\
\end{array}
$$

Even with long multiplication it is sensible to choose the simplest number as the multiplier. By selecting 333 it was only necessary to multiply once by 3. However, had 587 been chosen as the multiplier the example would have looked like this:

$$
\begin{array}{r}
333 \times 587 \\
587 \\
\hline
166,500 \\
26,640 \\
2,331 \\
\hline
195,471 \\
\end{array}
$$

which is rather more difficult to calculate.

5   Division

Division is the opposite of multiplication, so some of the methods for multiplication can be used in reverse.

(a)   DIVISION BY MULTIPLICATION

In order to divide by 5 it is possible to multiply by 2 and divide by 10. To divide by 10 the decimal point is moved up one place.
For example: $695 \div 5$

First multiply the dividend by 2: $695 \times 2 = 1,390$
Then divide the product by 10: $1,390 \div 10 = 139$

This method of doubling both dividend and divisor can be used in any situation where it is easier to divide by double the divisor. However, it is important to remember that any remainder will also be doubled.
For example: $243 \div 15$

Double both numbers: $\dfrac{486}{30} = 16$ remainder 6

The remainder must be halved so: $243 \div 15 = 16$ remainder 3

Sometimes it is more convenient to halve both dividend and divisor. In this event the remainder will be halved.
For example: $1,052 \div 16$

Halve both numbers: $\dfrac{526}{8} = 65$ remainder 6

Now double the remainder: $1,052 \div 16 = 65$ remainder   12

(b)   DIVISION BY FACTORS

If dividend and divisor include the same factors, one can divide by these to give a more manageable sum.
For example: $31,800 \div 420$

First divide by 10: $\dfrac{31,800}{420} = \dfrac{3,180}{42}$

Then by 2: $\dfrac{1,590}{21}$

Finally by 3: $\dfrac{530}{7} = 75$ remainder 5

However, should there be a remainder this must be multiplied back by all the divisors. So $5 \times 3 \times 2 \times 10 = 300$.
The answer to $31,800 \div 420$ is 75 remainder 300.

(c)   CALCULATIONS CONTAINING BOTH MULTIPLICATION AND DIVISION

These can usually be simplified by factorisation. When doing this it is sensible to reduce one of the numbers as far as possible, before looking for factors in another. This will reduce the amount of calculation. For example:

$$\frac{48 \times 345}{720}$$

First try to reduce the smallest number.
Divide both 48 and 720 by 12: $\qquad \dfrac{4 \times 345}{60}$

Then divide both 4 and 60 by 4: $\qquad \dfrac{1 \times 345}{15}$

Multiply both numbers by 2: $\qquad \dfrac{690}{30} = 23$

6   Notation

One of the most vital symbols in arithmetic and one of the most misused is the straight line. A single underlining means 'calculations have been performed above this line, the answer is underneath.' A double underlining means 'the figures above these lines have been dealt with and they are no longer to be taken into account.'
   A simple example will show the effect of this:

(a) Stock at start	56,000	Sales	500,000
(b) Purchases	379,000		
(c) Less stock on hand	(60,000)		
(d) Cost of sales	375,000		
(e) Gross profit	125,000		
(f)	500,000		500,000

Line (d) cost of sales has been calculated by casting lines (a), (b) and (c). Line (f) is the sum of lines (d) and (e). No further calculations are required after line (f).
   The above example may be contrasted with the following:

(a) Stock at start	56,000	Sales	500,000
(b) Purchases	379,000		
(c) Less stock on hand	(60,000)		
(d) Cost of sales	375,000		
(e) Gross profit	125,000		
(f)	500,000		500,000

The second example shows that line (f) on the left hand side has been calculated by casting lines (a) to (e), and is plainly incorrect as the answer to that is 875,000. Moreover further calculations are anticipated, and an answer is required to the sum on the right hand side.

7 Parts of a Number

A whole number may be divided into an infinite number of parts. These may be expressed in two forms as both fractions and decimals.

(a) FRACTIONS

A fraction is written in the same way as a division sum. $\frac{1}{2}$ or a half means that one unit has been divided into two parts.
$\frac{1}{4}$ or a quarter means that one unit has been divided into four parts.
$\frac{2}{5}$ means that two units have been divided into five parts.

The top number which represents the number of units is called the numerator. The bottom number which represents the number of parts into which it is to be divided is called the denominator.

As with all division sums, a fraction should be simplified as far as possible.

For example: $\frac{16}{64}$

Divide both numbers by 4: $\frac{4}{16}$

Divide by 4 again: $\frac{1}{4}$.

In a real or 'proper' fraction, the denominator is larger than the numerator. If the denominator is smaller than the numerator, then the fraction represents at least one whole number.

For example: $\frac{6}{5}$.

Divide 5 into 6 and the answer is 1, remainder 1.

The remainder also needs to be divided by 5 which equals $\frac{1}{5}$.

Thus $\frac{6}{5} = 1\frac{1}{5}$.

(i) *Addition and subtraction*
Fractions can only be added and subtracted when their denominators are the same.

So $\frac{1}{5} + \frac{2}{5} = \frac{3}{5}$.

When the denominators are not the same it is necessary to multiply the fraction to find a common denominator.

For example: $\dfrac{1}{5} + \dfrac{1}{3}$

Multiply the denominators together to find a common denominator:

$$5 \times 3 = 15$$

Then multiply the numerators by the same amount as the denominators.

$\dfrac{1}{5}$ multiply both numbers by 3 equals $\dfrac{3}{15}$

$\dfrac{1}{3}$ multiply both numbers by 5 equals $\dfrac{5}{15}$

$$\dfrac{3}{15} + \dfrac{5}{15} = \dfrac{8}{15}$$

(ii) *Multiplication and division*

Fortunately these are less cumbersome than addition and subtraction as it is not necessary to find a common denominator. Multiplication is most straightforward as the numerators are multiplied together to give a new numerator and the denominators to give a new denominator.

For example: $\dfrac{1}{5} \times \dfrac{1}{3} = \dfrac{1}{15}$.

$$\dfrac{2}{5} \times \dfrac{2}{3} = \dfrac{4}{15}.$$

A point to note is that the product of multiplication by fractions is smaller than either of the numbers multiplied. Division is performed in the same way as multiplication, only the divisor is turned upside down. For example:

$$\dfrac{1}{5} \div \dfrac{1}{3} = \dfrac{1}{5} \times \dfrac{3}{1} = \dfrac{3}{5}$$

$$\dfrac{2}{5} \div \dfrac{2}{3} = \dfrac{2}{5} \times \dfrac{3}{2} = \dfrac{6}{10} = \dfrac{3}{5}$$

A point to note is that the answer to a division of fractions is larger than either the divisor or the dividend.

The reason for this apparent reversal of the laws of nature becomes clear if the meaning of multiplication and division is considered. Instead of the multiplication sign the word 'of' is sometimes used. A fraction of a number is by definition smaller than the number, so a third of six will be smaller than six.

$$\dfrac{6}{1} \times \dfrac{1}{3} = \dfrac{6}{3} = 2$$

In fact, when multiplying by a third, one is really dividing by a three.

For the division of fractions the reverse is true.

It will be noted that all four arithmetical functions are quite complicated with fractions, and so the decimal representation of parts of a number is generally preferred. Indeed, in order to use a calculator it is necessary to convert fractions into decimals.

(b) DECIMALS

Fortunately, it is easy to do this conversion. A fraction is a division sum, a decimal is the answer.

A quarter may be written as $\frac{1}{4}$ or the sum may be completed

$$4 \overline{)1 \cdot 00000}$$
$$\underline{\cdot 25}$$

and a quarter represented as ·25. The dividing line between whole numbers and parts of numbers is marked by the decimal point. In this system the number nought has an important role to play. At the beginning of this chapter the importance of the position of the digit was discussed in hundreds, tens and units. This importance remains undiminished when considering parts of numbers. For example:

$$\frac{1}{10} = \cdot 1 \qquad \frac{1}{100} = \cdot 01 \qquad \frac{1}{1,000} = \cdot 001$$

This sequence can be obtained to infinity. The further a digit is from the right side of the decimal point the smaller it is. When multiplying decimals it is vital to remember that the product is less than either of the original numbers.

For example: $\cdot 2 \times \cdot 25$.

First consider 2×25 which equals 50.
Then count the number of digits to the right of the decimal point in both numbers. There are three, and so there must be three digits to the right of the decimal point in the answer.
$\cdot 2 \times \cdot 25 = \cdot 050$ which is usually written $\cdot 05$.

In division it is easier to find the right place for the decimal point. The answer to a division sum will remain the same if both divisor and dividend are multiplied by the same number. Therefore, multiply both numbers by whatever is necessary to make the divisor a whole number.
For example: $\cdot 2 \div \cdot 25$

To make the divisor into a whole number multiply by 100. This is done by moving the decimal point to the right two places.

$$20 \div 25 = \frac{20}{25} = \frac{4}{5} = \cdot 8$$

Some fractions do not work out exactly in decimals, for example a third and multiples of it; such figures are usually rounded at two or three places of decimals.

For example: $\dfrac{1}{3} = \cdot333$

$$\dfrac{2}{3} = \cdot667$$

8 Proportion

In order to compare one item with another it is necessary to have a common base. This may be done by considering the items as parts of a set and representing them as fractions with a common denominator, ratios, or in a more specialised way as fractions with a denominator of 100, percentages. For example, a factory employs a workforce of 1,000. Of these 625 are men and 375 women. This can be expressed as a fraction using the following formula:

$$\dfrac{\text{men}}{\text{total work force}} : \dfrac{\text{women}}{\text{total work force}}$$

$$\dfrac{625}{1,000} : \dfrac{375}{1,000} = \dfrac{5}{8} : \dfrac{3}{8}$$

which may be shown as a ratio of 5 men to 3 women. Alternatively, the calculation can stop when the common denominator reaches 100:

$$\dfrac{625}{1,000} : \dfrac{375}{1,000} = \dfrac{62\cdot5}{100} : \dfrac{37\cdot5}{100}$$

The proportion may then be written as: 62·5% of the workforce are men and 37·5% are women.

(a)   PERCENTAGES

A percentage has been defined as a fraction with a denominator of 100. To convert a fraction or a decimal to a percentage multiply by 100.

Example

$$\dfrac{1}{4} = \dfrac{1}{4} \times 100 = 25\%$$ $\cdot25 = \cdot25 \times 100 = 25\%$

$$\dfrac{1}{5} = \dfrac{1}{5} \times 100 = 20\%$$ $\cdot2 = \cdot2 \times 100 = 20\%$

$$\dfrac{7}{10} = \dfrac{7}{10} \times 100 = 70\%$$ $\cdot7 = \cdot7 \times 100 = 70\%$

To calculate the percentage of a quantity, reconvert the percentage to decimal or fraction and multiply.

Example

15% of $£20 = \cdot 15 \times £20 = £3$

20% of $£80 = \dfrac{20}{100} \times \dfrac{£80}{1} = £16$

This is the calculation required to find the amount of VAT to add to an invoice.

To calculate a quantity from a given percentage divide by the given percentage and multiply by 100.

Example

150 tons, which was 8 % of the stock, was damaged in a flood. What was the total stock?

$$\dfrac{150}{8} \times \dfrac{100}{1} = 1{,}875 \text{ tons.}$$

To express one quantity as a percentage of another, place the quantity to be expressed as a percentage, usually the smaller figure, over the quantity to which it is to be related and multiply by 100.

Example

During the year ended 31 December 19x9 the gross profit of a business was $£130{,}500$ and the sales were $£652{,}500$. What was the percentage of gross profit to sales?

$$\dfrac{130{,}500}{652{,}500} \times 100 = \dfrac{261}{1{,}305} \times 100 = \dfrac{1}{5} \times 100 = 20\%$$

The gross profit percentage was 20 %

VAT calculation

Most large invoices show the amount of Value Added Tax separately, but many invoices from retail stores only show the total amount of the bill inclusive of VAT. The invoice also shows the rate of VAT. As this VAT can be reclaimed by a business which is registered for the tax, it is necessary to extract the VAT paid and enter it separately in the petty cash book.

The invoice contains the cost of the goods	100 %
and VAT at the current rate, for instance	10 %
so the bill totals	110 %

Now it is possible to calculate the VAT.

Example

A bill inclusive of VAT at 10 % totals $£55$; calculate the VAT.

$£55$ equals 110 %, therefore the 10 % VAT equals $\dfrac{55}{110} \times 10 = £5$.

If the rate of VAT was 15 % the bill would total 115 %.

Example

A bill inclusive of VAT at 15% totals £23; calculate the VAT.

£23 equals 115%, therefore 15% VAT equals $\frac{23}{115} \times 15 = £3$

(b) RATIOS

A ratio can be found by the formula given at the beginning of this section, placing the items to be compared over the total sum of the items, or simply by direct comparison. Example: the current assets of a business were £50,000 and the current liabilities were £25,000. What was the ratio of current assets to current liabilities?

The ratio is 50,000 : 25,000 which can be reduced by division to a proportion of 2 : 1

Example

A business had current assets of £75,000 and fixed assets of £100,000. What was the ratio of current assets to fixed assets? The ratio is 75,000 : 100,000 which can be reduced by division to 3 : 4.

The decision whether to express proportion by percentage or by ratio will depend on what is customary for the items concerned. In any event it is extremely simple to convert ratios to percentages and vice-versa.

Example

Express the current assets from the last example as a percentage of the total assets. The ratio was 3 : 4. $3 + 4 = 7$ which is the common denominator.

Therefore the ratio can be expressed as $\frac{3}{7}$: $\frac{4}{7}$

The current assets are $\frac{3}{7}$ which is shown as a percentage by multiplying by 100.

$\frac{3}{7} \times 100 = 42 \cdot 85\%$

Current assets are 42·85% of total assets.

Example

From the last example in section 8a show the ratio of the gross profit to the sales. The gross profit was 20% of the sales.

This can be expressed as a fraction $\frac{1}{5}$.

This means that the ratio of gross profit to sales is 1 : 5.

Questions

1.1   Smith, Smith, Smith and Son are in partnership; the three Smiths own $\frac{1}{3}$, $\frac{3}{10}$ and $\frac{3}{20}$ of the capital of the business respectively. The capital totals £120,000. Calculate the capital owned by the partner with the smallest share in the business.

1.2   Three brothers called Tomb decide to purchase a funeral parlour. The eldest brother pays $\frac{4}{5}$, the second brother $\frac{1}{7}$ and the third brother the remainder of the cost price. The youngest brother paid £18,000; what was the cost of the business?

1.3   Super Stores has three departments, A, B, and C. The sales for the year ended December 31 are £64,000, £48,000 and £16,000 for each of the departments respectively. The expenses of the business for the year were as follows:

Wages and salaries	£ 7,200
Lighting and heating	2,000
Rent and rates	2,800
Insurance	1,200
Carriage	1,600
General expenses	960
Sundry expenses	240
	£16,000

Apportion each individual expense to the departments on the basis of sales.

1.4   Hydrogen Cars Ltd. has produced a budget for 19x3. In this a gross profit of £150,000 and a net profit of £75,000 are anticipated. Wages are estimated to be £40,000. Owing to economic pressure the company grants a wage increase of 20 %. Calculate the new budgeted wage figure and the revised net profit.

1.5   A firm wishes to produce a budget for the current year. The accountant estimates that business will remain at the same level as the previous year, but that an allowance must be made for inflation which is expected to run at 15 %. From the following list of last year's expenses, produce the budgeted expenses for the current year.

Wages and salaries	£10,000
Rent and rates	6,500
Lighting and heating	1,200
Motor expenses	1,300
Office expenses	800
Sundry expenses	200
	£20,000

1.6 An accounts clerk receives a salary of £3,500 a year. She has personal allowances of £1,300. If the basic rate of tax is 25%, how much tax will she pay in the year?

1.7 National Insurance contributions must be paid on all income. If the rate of contribution is 5% how much will a person earning £4,480 a year pay in National Insurance?

1.8 A company has sales of £225,000 and a gross profit of £45,000. Calculate the gross profit percentage.

1.9 A company has sales of £480,000 and a gross profit percentage of 25%. Calculate the gross profit.

1.10 A company has sales of £155,000 and a gross profit percentage of 30%. Calculate the gross profit.

1.11 A company has a gross profit of £163,000 and a gross profit percentage of 20%. Calculate the sales.

1.12 The rate of VAT is 15%. Calculate the VAT chargeable on the following invoices: £70, £55, £37, £1·20, £3·40, £6·20.

1.13 The rate of VAT is 12%. Calculate the VAT chargeable on goods sold for the following sums: £88, £64, £28, £3·20, £5·60, £0·72, £6.

1.14 The rate of VAT is 10%. Calculate the amount of VAT which has been included in the total of the following invoices: £110, £220, £341, £715, £3·30, £4·62, £6·93, £1·32.

1.15 The rate of VAT is 20%. Calculate the amount of VAT which has been included in the following invoices: £60, £240, £540, £768, £3·36, £4·62, £5·34, £0·66.

1.16 The rate of VAT is 25%. Calculate the amount of VAT which has been included in the following invoices: £50, £250, £745, £590, £6·75, £3·30, £1·55, £4·05.

1.17 The rate of VAT is 15%. Calculate the amount of VAT which has been included in the following invoices: £1,150, £345, £690, £138, £18·40, £10·35, £8·05, £5·75.

1.18   A salesman is paid a commission equal to 10% of the profit he earns for his employers after payment of the commission. He made a profit of £12,100 before his commission. How much did he receive?

1.19   A barman is paid 12½% of the bar profits after payment of his commission. The bar profits before his commission were £8,100. How much did he receive?

1.20   The current assets of a business are £75,000 and the current liabilities £25,000. What is the current ratio?

1.21   A business has fixed assets valued at £150,000 and current assets of £125,000. What is the ratio of current to fixed assets?

Chapter 2   ARITHMETIC 2   Roots and powers, simple equations, metric weights and measures, and currency conversion

1   Roots and Powers

These are simply a convenient method of expressing a number broken down into its factors.

The square of a number is that number multiplied by itself.

For example $2 \times 2 = 4$. 4 is the square of 2 and may be written as 2^2. This is called two to the power of two.

A number multiplied by itself is called a square because it can be represented diagramatically as a square:

```
      2  3  4  5
  O  O| O| O| O
  O  O| O| O| O
  O  O  O| O| O
  O  O  O  O| O
  O  O  O  O  O
```

It can be seen that:

$$3^2 = 9$$
$$4^2 = 16$$
$$5^2 = 25$$

Conversely, the square root of 4 is 2, the square root of 9 is 3, the square root of 16 is 4, and the square root of 25 is 5. This can be written as:

$$\sqrt{4} = 2 \qquad \sqrt{9} = 3 \qquad \sqrt{16} = 4 \qquad \sqrt{25} = 5$$

However, 4 is the square root of 16, but 2 is the square root of 4. This relationship can be expressed as 2 is the cube root of 16, and written as $\sqrt[3]{16} = 2$. The other way of looking at it is that $2 \times 2 \times 2 = 2^3 = 16$.

In order to multiply the same factor expressed to any power, one only has to add the powers.

For example: $2^3 \times 2^5 = 2^8$.

This can be proved by writing the calculation out in full:

$$\underbrace{2 \times 2 \times 2}_{2^3} \times \underbrace{2 \times 2 \times 2 \times 2 \times 2}_{2^5} = 2^8$$

The system of expressing a number composed of the same factors as a power of the factor is a form of shorthand. It is a convenient method of expressing very large numbers which are difficult to comprehend. For example:

$$18,446,744,073,709,551,616$$

is a rather large number; it is difficult to express it in words, and even more difficult to comprehend the quantity it is attempting to convey. However, it can be written more simply as 2^{64}.

A practical use for this is to express the capacity of a computer.

It is important to realise when dealing with powers that the increase by one power multiplies the answer by the factor. For example:

$$3^2 = 9 \quad \text{but} \quad 3^3 = 9 \times 3 = 27$$
$$2^3 = 16 \quad \text{but} \quad 2^4 = 16 \times 2 = 32$$

On the other hand, the decrease by one power divides the answer by the factor. For example:

2^{63} is half the large number given above, that is $9,223,372,036,854,775,808$

A further example can be given as a problem: a pernicious weed, escaped from a research laboratory, doubled in size every day. It took just twenty days to cover the nearby boating lake. How long would two of the same plants take to cover a similar sized lake? Ponder the question before arriving at a conclusion. Since the weed doubles in size daily on the nineteenth day it must cover only half the lake. Therefore, two weeds would take nineteen days to cover the lake.

(a)   FINDING SQUARE ROOTS

Sometimes it is possible to break down the number into factors which are well-known squares. For example:

$\sqrt{144} = \sqrt{16} \times \sqrt{9} = 4 \times 3 = 12$

$16 \times 9 = 144$

However, this can be time-consuming and will only work for certain numbers. There is a long method for calculating square roots, but it is unnecessary to use such methods, as there are excellent square root tables and most calculators have a square root facility.

Nevertheless, should a number conveniently be expressed as a power of a factor, the square root can be found by halving the power. For example:

$$\sqrt{2^4} = 2^2 \quad \sqrt{16} = 4$$
$$\sqrt{2^6} = 2^3 \quad \sqrt{64} = 8$$

2 Simple Equations

Knowledge of how to use simple equations can help in solving not only the brain-twisters in the Sunday papers but also some more practical problems.

(a) ALGEBRA

Many problems in which an unknown quantity is to be discovered can be solved by the use of algebra. All algebra does is to substitute letters for the unknown quantity or quantities, and this enables calculations to progress. Not all problems can be solved by means of algebra; sometimes there is insufficient information, but a great many can be solved with a little elementary knowledge. There is one golden rule in algebra: DO NOT DIVIDE BY NOUGHT. If this is done the answer will be nonsensical. The reason for this is that any number divided by nought equals nought.

Example

	$x = y$
Multiply by 2	$2x = 2y$
Move all figures to one side	$2x - 2y = 0$
Add $2x - 2y$ to both sides	$2x - 2y + (2x - 2y) = (2x - 2y)$
which can be written as	$4(x - y) = 2(x - y)$
Divide both sides by $x - y$	$4 = 2$

This answer is clearly wrong. The error lay in dividing by $x - y$, since $x = y$ and so the divisor was nought.

Nevertheless, the ability to prove that $4 = 2$ is not without advantages; bets have been laid about more trivial matters.

(b) SOLVING SIMPLE PROBLEMS

To solve a problem with an unknown quantity, let x represent the unknown, but be quite specific as to whether x represents pounds, pence, miles or anything else. If the problem contains fractions, multiply both sides by a common multiple to clear them.

Isolate the terms containing x to one side of the equation. Divide throughout by the number of x's.

Example

A bus company operates a flat-rate fare of 25 pence within the city. Pensioners pay a reduced fare of 15 pence. One Monday 600 tickets were issued and the total receipts were £110. The company wishes to know how many pensioners travelled that day in order to claim a subsidy from local government.

Let the number of pensioners be x, and the number of other passengers be y.

The total number of travellers was 600	$x + y = 600$
The total number of pence received in both 15 and 25 pence fares was 11,000.	$15x + 25y = 11{,}000$
To eliminate the y's, multiply the first equation by 25	$25x + 25y = 15{,}000$
Subtract the second equation from this answer	$10x = 4{,}000$
Divide by the number of x's	$x = 400$

The number of pensioners who travelled on Monday was 400. This answer can be checked. If there were 400 pensioners there must have been 200 other passengers.

$400 \times 15p + 200 \times 25p = £60 + £50 = £110$, which was the takings for the day.

3 Metric Weights and Measures

The metric system is simple and has none of the complications of the imperial system. The only problem that may arise is if an order is made verbally for a 'ton' of a commodity and there is misunderstanding whether a metric 'tonne' or an imperial 'ton' is required. As an imperial ton is some forty pounds or eighteen kilograms heavier than a metric tonne this may make a considerable difference on a large order, especially where a price has been quoted.

The main metric weights are:
gram	
kilogram	1,000 grams
tonne	1,000 kilograms.

One kilogram equals 2·2 pounds.

The main metric measures are:
millimetre	·001 metres
centimetre	·01 metres
metre	
kilometre	1,000 metres

One metre equals 39·37 inches.

Before doing any calculations with metric units it is essential to convert all the figures into one common unit.

Example

What is the sum of 27·6 m, 19·5 cms. and 50,560 mms?

Convert all the figures to metres: 27·6

$$\begin{array}{r} 27 \cdot 6 \\ \cdot 195 \\ 50 \cdot 560 \\ \hline 78 \cdot 355 \text{ metres.} \end{array}$$

4 Currency Conversion

The major currencies of the world are decimal, which makes conversion simple. The rate of exchange between currencies fluctuates from day to day, and even during the day. Current rates are published in the national papers, but if a large purchase of currency is contemplated it is sensible to obtain a current quotation.

Example

$£1 = 3·72$ Swiss francs

Convert £20 into Swiss francs.

$£1 = 3·72$ Swiss francs

$£20 = 20 \times 3·72 = 74·4$ Swiss francs.

Convert 100 Swiss francs into sterling.

$$1 \text{ Swiss franc} = £\ \frac{1}{3·72} = £·2688$$

$$100 \text{ Swiss francs} = £26·88$$

An important point when drawing up accounts in two currencies simultaneously, which is quite common when a business is a subsidiary of an overseas company, is to remember which currency is being dealt with. This rather obvious precaution has been overlooked in the past, with catastrophic results.

5 Vocabulary

A million = 1,000,000: on this everyone is agreed.

A billion = 1,000,000,000, or a thousand million according to the Americans, and usually the British when referring to money (*Note 1*)

= $1,000,000^2$ or a million million according to the *Oxford Dictionary*, and most British people when not referring to money (*Note 2*)

A trillion = $1,000,000^2$ or a million million in circumstances as *Note 1*.

= $1,000,000^3$ or a million million million in circumstances as *Note 2*.

This can cause a good deal of misunderstanding. If there is any doubt as to the exact meaning of the term it is sensible to obtain clarification, especially as such large sums are involved.

Questions

2.1 A mad, but brilliant scientist produces a strain of killer bees. They reproduce daily and can breed twenty-four hours after birth. Dr. Doom threatens to release two of these daily unless he receives a million pounds. How many bees will be flying free after seven days?*

2.2 Two cousins Michael and Roy were travelling with their grandmother. Michael had brought 5 bars of chocolate and Roy 3. They shared these equally among the three of them. When they arrived home their grandmother gave them a box of 8 coloured crayons, and told them to divide the crayons between them in proportion to their contribution of chocolate. How many crayons should each boy have?*

2.3 C. Sellars Ltd. are having a sales promotion in an attempt to sell more tights. They advertise 'free' tights and the system works in the following way. Each customer must buy eleven packets of tights direct from Sellars for £10. The customer then sells ten packets to friends at £1 each and is left with a free packet of tights. She sends the names and addresses of her ten customers to Sellars, and he invites them to purchase a further eleven packets of tights and to sell ten.

Assuming a 100% response rate and a week between the delivery of each new batch of tights, how many packets of tights will be sold in six weeks from one original customer?*

2.4 Connie Merchant starts a business retailing French perfume by mail order. The business is not a success, so to promote custom she initiates a new system. She advertises a free gift of perfume valued at £1. A customer must send £10; for this she will receive ten vouchers for perfume of £1 each and her free perfume. She must sell the vouchers to her friends and receive back her money. The purchasers of the vouchers must send the voucher and £9 to receive their free perfume and ten further vouchers.

Assuming 100% response rate and a week between the delivery of each new batch of perfume and vouchers:
  (a) How much money will Connie receive after five weeks from one initial customer?
  (b) How many bottles of perfume will she have dispatched?
  (c) Why do you think that this method of selling, known as pyramid selling, is illegal in Great Britain?*

* Answers are given on p 34.

2.5 A charity decided to have a fund-raising campaign. A hundred parcels were sent out to well-wishers. The parcels contained a request for £1 donation and ten packets to distribute to friends. Each packet contained the same request and a further ten packets to distribute. This continued for five further rounds.

Assuming a 100% success rate:
(a) How much would the charity receive?
(b) What would be the problem in the United Kingdom if the request were to continue into the sixth round?*

2.6 A small local charity decided to raise funds by means of a series of coffee mornings. An initial fifty people were invited to a coffee morning. All paid 25 pence for their coffee, and promised to invite a further six people to a similar coffee morning of their own. The six invitees then paid 25 pence for the coffee, and promised to invite five people to morning coffee on the same basis. The scheme continued until on the final round only one person was invited to coffee. All funds were donated to the charity.

Assuming 100% response rate:
(a) How much would the charity receive?
(b) What practical problems would arise if this scheme were initiated in a town with a population of 100,000?*

2.7 A professor leaves Bristol at 10 a.m. to give a lecture at London University. He drives at a sensible 60 mph. Half an hour later his wife discovers his briefcase and lecture notes, and follows him in her sports car. In her concern she travels at 90 mph. If she is not stopped for speeding, at what time will she catch her husband?*

2.8 A train is timetabled to complete a 60-mile journey in 72 minutes. After travelling a certain time on schedule it is delayed for five minutes by falling leaves and has to travel at 60 mph to complete the journey on time. At what distance from the destination were the falling leaves?*

2.9 A British Airways jet is scheduled to complete a journey in $4\frac{1}{2}$ hours travelling at 600 mph. It meets with turbulence and has to touch down to refuel which takes half an hour. To complete the journey on time it would have to travel at twice its initial speed. The fastest it can actually fly is 750 mph. If it achieves this speed how late will it be on arrival?*

2.10 To encourage the use of public transport during off-peak hours, the bus company offers pensioners a reduced flat rate fare of 20 pence between 10 a.m. and 4 p.m. The normal flat rate fare is 50% higher.

Previously the daily receipts during that period were £150. The number of pensioners travelling doubles and there is an increase in receipts of £20 a day. How many of the passengers who travelled regularly prior to the concession being offered were pensioners?*

---

* Answers are given on p 34.

2.11 Exchange rates to the pound are as follows:

Belgium 65 francs.

Germany 4 marks.

Japan 555 yen.

U.S.A. $2·3.

(a) Convert £150 into Belgian francs.
(b) Convert $1,000 U.S. into German marks.
(c) Convert 1,000 German marks into yen.
(d) Convert 100,000 yen into pounds sterling.

Answers to Questions, Chapter 2

2.1 $2^7 + 2^6 + 2^5 + 2^4 + 2^3 + 2^2 + 2 = 2^8 - 2 = 254$ bees.

2.2 Everyone consumed $\frac{3}{4}$ bars of chocolate. Michael gave $\frac{1}{4}$ to his grandmother from his 5 bars, and Roy gave $\frac{1}{4}$ from his 3 bars. Michael should have 7 crayons and Roy only 1.

2.3 $11(1 + 10 + 10^2 + 10^3 + 10^4 + 10^5) = 11(111,111) = 1,222,221$ packets of tights.

2.4 (a) Connie's receipts are $£9 (10 + 10^2 + 10^3 + 10^4) + 10$
$= 9 (11,110) + 10$
$= £100,000.$

(b) Connie has dispatched 11,111 bottles of perfume valued at £1.

(c) There are 100,000 vouchers out each purporting to be worth £1, but these can only be used by paying a further £9 and making a commitment to sell 10 more vouchers. It seems unlikely that buyers will be found for these so a high proportion of the vouchers are valueless.

2.5 (a) The charity would receive $100 (1 + 10 + 10^2 + 10^3 + 10^4 + 10^5) = £11,111,100.$

(b) By the sixth round some 111,111,100 people would be involved: the population of the United Kingdom is around 55 million.

2.6 (a) The charity would receive 97,850 contributions of 25 pence, that is £24,462.50.

(b) 97,850 need to be involved in the scheme; a town with a population of 100,000 has only about 25,000 families and a considerable proportion of these will be children.

2.7 11.30 a.m.

2.8 25 miles.

2.9 18 minutes.

2.10 200 pensioners.

Chapter 3   THE DEVELOPMENT AND PURPOSE OF ACCOUNTING

1   History

Since trade commenced man has recorded his transactions. The earliest accounts have been found inscribed on tablets of stone in the ruins of Babylon, while the Incas of Peru recorded their financial dealings on knotted lengths of string called 'quipus'.

Just as the roots of the European languages spread from the cultivated sub-continent of India to the barbaric West, so the basis of our present mathematical system came from the Middle East and Northern Africa. The earliest accounts were little more than a record of receipts and payments kept in a cash book, with possibly a file of bills. Nevertheless, they still make interesting reading. The Domesday Book was prepared to enable William the Conqueror to tax the English, and so was a basic accounting record. Private household accounts can give a clear insight into the domestic and business life of people centuries ago.

It is not known when the method of double entry book-keeping, now universally employed, was first introduced. The earliest extant record of this system in operation dates from 1340 in Genoa, but as it shows a highly developed system presumably the origins of the method are considerably further back. However, the system flourished in Italy; an early text book describing double entry was written by an Italian, Lucas Pacioli and dates from 1494. So this book follows in a long and honourable tradition. The Medici used double entry book-keeping to control their vast commercial and banking interests in Florence during the fifteenth century. One can imagine the many and varied entries in the ledger accounts for poisons.

Double entry book-keeping records the twofold aspect of every transaction. When a person puts capital into a business he parts with his goods or money and the business receives them; when goods are sold on credit to a customer the business parts with its stock and gains a debtor. Both aspects of these transactions are recorded in the principal book of account, the ledger. The mechanics of the entries are dealt with in detail in Chapter 4.

Accounting theory continued to develop, especially in Italy and Germany. In 1586 Don Pietro added to it his concept of a separate business entity. This was to reach its final flowering in the concept of a company as a separate legal entity, divorced from both its owners and its directors, who merely act on its behalf. It was the industrial revolution which sparked off a general interest in accounting procedures, formerly confined to bankers and other moneylenders. Agricultural communities throughout the world have been forced to adapt. It is no longer sufficient to see a flock of sheep or herd of cows fattening under one's eyes, in order to know whether one is making a profit. It is necessary to record expenditure, to keep a note of money owed by debtors, and to whom money is owed and by when it must be repaid.

Moreover, with the advent of large industrial concerns, parties other than the owners of the business have a direct interest in its financial affairs. These are the creditors and moneylenders mentioned above, and the Inland Revenue. Bob Cratchit scratched away with his quill to satisfy the accounting requirements of Scrooge, but modern inventions have taken the drudgery out of book-keeping.

The principal book of account is the ledger. Originally it was a leather-bound tome written up by hand, and perhaps in a larger business divided into several volumes dealing with different sections of the enterprise. The nominal ledger records all the items of income and expense; the sales ledger details debtors accounts; the purchase ledger details creditors accounts; and the cash book contains all money transactions. The same main divisions are still made but the form of the ledger may vary considerably. It may be hand-written but in a loose-leaf binder, which means that precautions must be taken to ensure no pages are mislaid or substituted. There are various simple forms of mechanised accounting in common use. The basis of these is sets of cards, each set representing a section of the ledger. Entries are made on the cards by an accounting machine in the same way as a typewriter, but the machine can total the entries. The cards are stored in special metal trays and again safeguards are required against loss and substitution. Even when cards are used the cash book is usually in the traditional form.

The computer is a major tool in the keeping of accounts, and its use is increasing rapidly with the introduction of the silicon chip which means that computers of small physical dimensions can have a large calculating and storage facility. When a computer is used the ledger is seen as a paper print-out, usually in sections which can be bound together month by month. Data to produce the ledger is stored on magnetic discs or tapes. The computer generally receives new information in the form of punched cards. It is obviously of vital importance to ensure that the new information given to the computer is accurate as any error will be reproduced in the ledger accounts.

The advantage of a computer is that it can process a large quantity of material very speedily and without error. The potential danger is that it is possible to rewrite the accounts completely, in a way which would be impossible by any other method because of the sheer volume of work involved. Computers also have the ability to print out information which is not included in the total figures; to include figures in the totals which are not printed out; to perform given exercises and then forget about them; and to do nearly anything else they may be programmed to do. This being so, there is considerable scope for fraud, and it is of great importance that safeguards are included in the basic computer programmes, that access to the computer functions is restricted, and that checks are made on a regular basis by an independent party.

It may be thought that, as the computer will make all the book-keeping entries, it is unnecessary for people to learn the steps of basic double entry. On the contrary, it is all the more essential to understand the principles thoroughly. A computer is an excellent machine for calculation and logical deduction but it lacks intuition as it cannot make arbitary connections. It makes a good servant when understood and utilised to the full, and comprehension is necessary if one is to make full use of the available power.

A study of systematically recorded accounts can help one to understand economics, but common sense and some acquaintance with history will also be an advantage. It is interesting to recall that when Italy was suffering from a cycle of boom and recession in the fifteenth century, the town of Florence introduced a new gold-based coin called the florin. This rapidly gained acceptance and superseded the other dubious currency then in circulation. The majority of nations left the gold standard during the twentieth century, which means that the world's currencies are not backed by gold or indeed any other stable asset, and that paper money can be printed by governments at their own discretion. The world economy as a whole is unstable and suffers the reverses of boom and recession. The reasons for this are complex and are argued about frequently and loudly by leading economists of different persuasions, but it might not be too much to suggest that inherently unstable currencies are at least a contributory factor in the cycle.

Sound book-keeping alone will not ensure the success of a commercial venture. The Medici of the Renaissance used double entry book-keeping, but made the unwise move of lending money to both sides in the war between England and France. Political loans are not as safe as sound commercial ones and the victorious Edward III defaulted on his debt, to the consternation of those who had supported him.

There is considerable risk in speculating in goods which have no intrinsic worth. Many claims are made for the potential capital appreciation of various items such as stamps, china and antiques. However, a salutary lesson can be learned from the tulips of Amsterdam. Dutch bulbs have been famous for many centuries, but at one time the price started to spiral upwards. Many rushed to buy the limited number of tulip bulbs available, the price increased still higher and great fortunes were made overnight. This was no South Sea Bubble; the investment was considered respectable, and banks even accepted bulbs as security for loans. There is a story that a visiting foreign dignitary actually ate some priceless bulbs, mistaking them for onions, to the despair of his host. It could not last; the bottom fell out of the market, many were ruined and the Dutch economy was left in a shambles.

2 Purpose

A business exists in order to make a profit, and the aim of the accounts is to show whether the business is doing this, and to give the managers information from which to make plans to increase this profitability.

To formulate policy managers need to know details of the various factors governing the success of a business. Such factors include sales, cost of sales and expenses. Accounts may be arranged to suit the particular needs of a business, but there are certain standard formats which are dealt with in this book.

Policy decisions must be made on all aspects of the business.

PRICING

If a business is selling a unique product it may be possible to raise prices considerably before demand slackens. However, if a business has competitors, customers will buy from the cheapest source, and in these circumstances it may be advantageous to lower prices in order to increase sales.

CONTROL OF DEBTORS AND CREDITORS

It is important to ensure that debtors pay within a reasonable period of time and that adequate steps are taken to chase defaulters; on the other hand, it may be financially advantageous to refrain from paying creditors until the last possible moment. However, this advantage must be weighed against that of maintaining a good working relationship with the firm's suppliers, in order to secure regular deliveries even in a time of shortages.

EXPENSES

A detailed breakdown of expenses is needed to ensure that these are strictly controlled and kept to a minimum. Study of the accounts will also inform management if loans or additional capital are required so that these can be arranged well in advance.

Other parties have an interest in the financial state of a business: these include the creditors, who wish to make sure they will be paid; moneylenders who also want to be repaid with interest in due course; government bodies who desire taxes; and employees and trade unions who need information to help them in their wage negotiations.

These parties have such very diverse interests that it might be sensible to draw up different sets of accounts to satisfy them. For example, when a bank manager is considering the grant of a loan to a firm, he is concerned over the security of the money: for this he looks to the assets and wishes to value them at their market value. The owners of the business, on the other hand, are not particularly interested in the market value of the assets, unless they wish to sell them, but want to spread the cost of the assets over their lifetime. Nevertheless, under the present system only one set of accounts is produced and it must be used in all circumstances. It is vital that all parties have confidence in the accounts and know that they conform to certain standards, so certain concepts and conventions are implicit in the preparation of accounts.

3 Concepts and Conventions

If accounts are to be useful it is imperative that the users can rely on them. For this reason auditors give a certificate that accounts show a 'true and fair view'. However, there are also certain concepts and conventions implicit in the preparation of accounts. Accounting is a developing subject and these concepts and conventions are continually being discussed and modified. Concepts are basic ideas, fundamental to the preparation of accounts, which have evolved over the centuries. A convention is an agreed method of dealing with these concepts.

THE CONCEPT OF DOUBLE ENTRY

Book-keeping records the dual aspect of every transaction, in that in every transaction one party gives and another receives. So, if a business sells goods, it parts with the goods but receives cash in exchange. This method of book-keeping leads to books which 'balance', as the 'giving' or credit entries equal the 'receiving' or debit entries; and to a statement of financial affairs termed a balance sheet, as the assets of a business are shown as owing to, or being owned by, the proprietors of the business.

The equation is:

$$\text{Capital} = \text{Assets} - \text{Liabilities}$$

THE CONCEPT OF THE SEPARATE BUSINESS ENTITY

A business is considered to be entirely separate from and independent of its owner. This is so even when a business is run by a sole proprietor. His private affairs must not be confused with his business dealings. Money that he takes from the business for private expenditure is a reduction of the capital of the business. If the business is short of cash and the owner pays a bill out of his private funds, this increases the capital of the business.

This concept was first proposed by Don Pietro in 1586 and so is of respectable antiquity.

39

THE GOING CONCERN CONCEPT

A business is assumed to have an infinite life, unless there is reason to believe it may soon be terminated. This means that assets can be valued at cost rather than at their break-up value which may well be considerably lower. For example a process plant refining sugar may have very complex and expensive machinery which is essential to the business, yet it may have no other use and in the event of a liquidation be sold for scrap.

Because this concept is fundamental to the preparation of accounts, if auditors have reason to believe that a company may not survive they will qualify their audit report with words to the effect that the accounts only show a 'true and fair' view of the financial state of the company if the business remains a going concern. That is, if attention is drawn to the matter in the accounts, there is cause for concern about the business.

THE ACCRUAL CONCEPT

Accounts show more than the receipts and payments of cash. Expenditure is matched with income for the period covered by the accounts. For example, if rent has been paid in advance or if amounts are due for fuel or telephone, appropriate adjustments are made to the accounts.

THE REALISATION CONCEPT

Profit is regarded as being realised at the point of sale. Unrealised profits may not be taken into account. The point of sale is normally when goods are removed to give effect to the transaction, but may be when the goods are invoiced and paid for if this occurs earlier. The point of sale does not depend on the date of ordering, the date of contract, or the date of payment.

THE MONEY MEASUREMENT CONCEPT

Accounts are restricted to the financial transactions of the business: they show only those items which can be recorded in terms of money. Other factors which may be essential to the success of the business are ignored. For example, the health of the owner or managing director, the strength of the management team and whether a key figure is about to resign, the skills and homogeneous working of artisans and craftsmen, and whether relations with the unions are harmonious. So the accounts do not give a complete picture of the state of a business.

THE COST CONCEPT

All transactions are entered in the books at cost. This does not necessarily reflect their true worth, but is done to achieve some measure of objectivity in the presentation of accounts. Over a period of time certain adjustments can be made; for example, if stock purchased for resale has lost value owing to market conditions, the lower value must be substituted.

Unfortunately, this concept implies a certain stability in the value of money. If a currency is suffering from rampant inflation, then historic cost accounts give rather peculiar results. For instance, a business purchased a factory on an industrial estate for £25,000. Ten years later it purchased the identical factory next door for £50,000. The business now shows the two factories on its books at an historic cost of £75,000, valuing one of the identical pair at twice the amount of the other. There are methods of adjusting accounts to allow for the effects of inflation but these are outside the scope of this book.

THE CONVENTION OF CONSISTENCY

The concepts give the underlying philosophy of accounting, but are capable of different interpretations. In order that the results of a business may be compared from year to year it is important that a suitable interpretation is decided upon and then adhered to. The aim of accounts is to show as true a position of the financial situation as possible, and the same treatment is not necessarily suitable for a large manufacturing concern and a small retail business. However, it is vital that the accounts are prepared on a consistent basis. This does not mean that a business can never change its accounting methods, but that such changes must be infrequent, carefully considered, and the effect of any change noted in the accounts.

THE CONVENTION OF MATERIALITY

An accounting system must justify its existence by producing useful, practical information at a reasonable cost. It is a servant of management, not its master. To itemise the unused paper clips in an office conforms to the letter of the accounting concepts but is singularly pointless. Assets that have a long life but little value can be written off in the accounts, and it is unnecessary to record in detail every item of petty expense; these can be recorded under the general heading of miscellaneous.

Businesses often make internal rules as to what they consider to be material. A large multinational company may well be able to ignore expenditure of several hundred pounds, which would be a substantial sum to a small retailer.

THE CONVENTION OF PRUDENCE

Also known as the conservatism convention. An accountant will take a prudent, not to say pessimistic view of future financial prospects. Only realised profits may be included in the accounts as stated in the concept of realisation: moreover, where there is a choice of methods of valuation the accountant will take the lower value. He will also make allowance for any possible losses.

Chapter 4 DOUBLE ENTRY

1(a) Definition

The Double Entry system of book-keeping is one whereby two entries are made for every transaction.

1(b) Explanation

Entries recording transactions are made in the Ledger which is the principal book of account. As mentioned in the previous chapter it is not necessarily a single book. It may be a set of books or cards or computer discs and print-out, all of which contain the same information although it may be presented in a slightly different way in each. However, in order to practise book-keeping ledger paper will be required. The following headed sheet shows the use of the various columns. It will be noted that the right hand side is merely a duplicate of the left.

Ledger Paper

Dr. Date	Details	Ref. No.	Amount	Date	Details	Ref. No.	Cr Amount

2 Book-keeping

This should become clear through the following illustration:
On April 1 Ernie Enterprise started a small second-hand car business. He went to see an accountant.

April 1   He put £1,000 into the business.
April 5   Bought two Ford Escorts at a car auction for £600.
April 8   Sold one car for £430.
April 15   Advertised in local paper £1.
April 17   Sold remaining car for £450.

Keen to make use of his recent business studies qualification, Ernie opened a loose-leaf ledger and made the entries as they occurred.

Dr.		Cash Account			Cr.
		£			£
April 1 Capital		1,000	April 5 Purchases		600
April 8 Sales		430	April 15 Advertising		1
April 17 Sales		450			

	Capital Account	
	April 1 Cash	1,000

Purchases Account		
April 5 Cash (2 cars)	600	

	Sales Account	
	April 8 Cash (1 car)	430
	April 17 Cash (1 car)	450

Expenses Account		
April 15 Cash (Advertising)	1	

It will be noted that there are only five transactions, but ten entries in the ledger. It will also be noted that each transaction appears on both sides of the ledger. There is one entry on the debit (left hand) side and a corresponding one opposite and equal on the credit (right hand) side. This illustrates the prime rule of double entry book-keeping: *For every debit there is a credit.*

Further analysis of the above example will show how this works.

2(a)   £1,000 INTO THE BUSINESS

Cash in the business increases by £1,000.
The Cash account must show the money coming in.
Since we debit what comes in, the cash account shows £1,000 on the dèbit side.
There must be a corresponding credit entry somewhere.
The money belongs to Ernie Enterprise so it might be possible to open an account in his name, but as he is the proprietor of the business it is customary to call the money Capital and place it in the Capital account. The entry in the capital account is a credit not merely in order to be opposite to the first debit entry but also because we credit what goes out and Ernie has paid out his money to the business.

2(b)   BOUGHT TWO CARS FOR £600

Cash goes out of the business.
Credit what goes out.
Credit cash account £600.
There must be a corresponding debit entry.
Goods bought for resale are known as purchases, so a purchase account is opened and a debit entry made of £600 to show the cars coming into the business.

2(c)   SOLD A CAR FOR £430

Cash comes into the busines, a car goes out of the business. The cash account is debited with £430.
There must be a corresponding credit entry.
A salès account is opened and credited with £430.

2(d)   ADVERTISED: COST £1

Cash goes out of the business and a service is received.
The cash account is credited with £1.
There must be a corresponding debit entry.
Advertising is an expense of the business so an expenses account is opened and debited with £1.

2(e)   SOLD CAR FOR £450

Entries as in (c) above.
Debit cash £450.
Credit sales £450.

3 Rules of Double Entry

(a) For every DEBIT there must be a CREDIT.

(b) Debit what comes in, Credit what goes out.

Further explanation of above:

Accounts must be DEBITED with:

Money received by the business.

Assets received by the business.

Services received and expenses incurred by the business.

Money owed to the business (Debtors)

Accounts must be CREDITED with:

Money paid by the business.

Assets sold by the business.

Services rendered by the business.

Money owed by the business (Creditors).

Income and profits of the business.

It must be noted that Debit and Credit in accountancy have a specific meaning which is not necessarily the same as their meaning in normal speech.

It must also be noted that the entries made in the Cash account are on the opposite side to the entries on a Bank statement. This can be confusing. The reason for this will be explained in a later chapter.

4(a) The Advantages of Double Entry

Double entry appears to make a lot more work. There is a proliferation of entries. Is any advantage gained from this or is it just part of a government job creation scheme? In earlier days a simple list of receipts and payments may have been sufficient but now the burden of taxation and the imposition of VAT (Value Added Tax) make the keeping of detailed records necessary for even the smallest business. There are five positive advantages:

(i) It provides a complete record of all transactions entered into by the business.

(ii) As there is a debit for every credit it is possible to make an arithmetical check on the accuracy of the entries.

(iii) It is a simple matter to draw up a Profit and Loss account.

(iv) A Balance Sheet can be prepared for any given date.

(v) It makes it easier to detect errors and fraud.

4(b) Expansion of the Above Advantages

(i) This is self-explanatory.

(ii) Arithmetical check: it is possible to make one complete list of the debits and another of the credits. The totals of the two lists should be equal.

From the above example:

List of debits	Cash	£1,000
		430
		450
	Purchases	600
	Expenses	1
		£2,481
List of credits	Cash	£ 600
		1
	Capital	1,000
	Sales	430
		450
		£2,481

(iii) Profit and Loss account ⎫ These will be dealt with in later
(iv)   Balance Sheet   ⎬ chapters
(v)   Detection of errors and fraud: this is made easier by both the complete record and the possibility of arithmetical check. Fraud may even by prevented by dividing the ledger so that any one person has access to only a portion of it. It then becomes very difficult to make fraudulent entries without being detected immediately.

5   Technical Terms

Asset
This is a possession of the business e.g. money, stock, land and buildings, plant and machinery, debtors (that is money owed to the business).

Liability
This is a debt owed by the business e.g. a bank overdraft, a loan, creditors.

Profit
This is a monetary gain to the business caused by the sale of goods or provision of services for more than their cost.

Loss
This may be caused by the sale of goods or services for less than their cost to the business, by the destruction or theft of uninsured assets, or by debtors failing to pay sums due.

Posting
This means entering transactions in the ledger from a book of prime entry or a source document. It is also used to refer to completing the double entry when one side has already been entered.

Casting
This means adding a column of figures, which may include negative numbers.

6 Types of Accounts in the Ledger

There are two main classes of accounts, personal and impersonal.

The personal accounts comprise the capital, debtors and creditors accounts. They are so named because the amounts therein relate to individuals.

The impersonal accounts may be subdivided into: real and nominal. Real accounts relate to assets—for example: premises, motor cars, and cash.

Nominal accounts deal with those items which have to be taken into account when computing the profit or loss that a business has made, for example: sales, purchases, rent, electricity.

7 Summary

(a)   For every debit there must be a credit.
(b)   Debit what comes in, credit what goes out.
(c)   Advantages of double entry:

    (i)   Complete record.
   (ii)   Arithmetical check.
  (iii)   Profit and loss account.
  (iv)   Balance sheet.
   (v)   Detection of errors and fraud.

Questions

Before attempting a question, decide which accounts are needed. It is advisable to start with the cash account, as all transactions will be recorded there at this stage.

4.1 *Jan. 1* Sid Brown started a newsagents. He put £1,500 into the business.
Jan. 3 Bought goods for resale £845.
Jan. 4 Day's takings £25.
Jan. 5 Paid rent for premises of £250.
Jan. 7 Takings for last three days £215.
Open a ledger for Sid Brown and make the entries to record the above transactions.

4.2 Bertrand Brunel decided to start a bridge-building business. He went to see a solicitor.
June 1 He was offered a contract to build a bridge over the Severn.
He put £5,000 of own money into the enterprise.
June 2 Purchased steel girders £2,000. Agreed to employ Dan at £60 per week.
June 3 Bought sundry other materials £1,250.
Paid for hire of small hut in which to shelter £25.
Paid for coffee, sugar and primus stove £5.
June 6 Received advance of £3,500, paid Dan his weekly wages.
Open a ledger and make the appropriate entries for the first week of business.

4.3 Without actually opening the ledger accounts, show where you would make entries to record the following transactions.

Dr.   Cr.

(a) Boat builder buys stationery for cash.
(b) Stationer's shop buys stationery in bulk for resale.
(c) Bob buys coffee for office use.
(d) Coffee Unlimited buys coffee beans from Brazil to retail in Europe paying cash.
(e) I.M. Retail finds that his till has taken £95 during the day.
(f) A retailer of electrical goods sells two televisions and a set of heated rollers in the pre-Christmas rush.
(g) A firm of accountants sells an antiquated typewriter by advertising in the local paper.
(h) The above firm pays for the advertising.

4.4 State five advantages of double entry book-keeping.

4.5 What do you understand by the term double entry book-keeping?

Chapter 5   THE TRIAL BALANCE

1(a)   Definition

A trial balance is an arithmetical test that the double entry has been completed in the ledger.

1(b)   Explanation

Before one proceeds to the final accounts and discovers whether the business has made a profit or a loss, it is essential to check that the double entry has been completed in the ledger. If it has not the accounts will be wrong. In a short example such as is used for practice in this book it is possible to make a quick visual check. However, this is quite impossible in a real ledger and it is necessary to practise the correct method.

2   Book-keeping

It is not necessary to make a list of all the entries in the ledger: a list of the balances on each account is all that is required.

At the end of his first period of trading Ernie Enterprise balanced his accounts and extracted a trial balance.

(a)   He looked at the cash account: a quick glance told him that the debits exceeded the credits. This is how it should be in the case of cash. Therefore, he totalled the debits and put the same total in the credit side. He made sure that he had left enough space to complete the missing entry on the credit side—and that the two totals were on a line with each other.

Dr.			Cash Account		Cr.
April 1	Capital	1,000	April 5	Purchases	600
April 8	Sales	430	April 15	Advertising	1
April 17	Sales	450			
	Total	£1,880			£1,880

Obviously there is a missing balance on the credit side and this must be $1,880 - (600 + 1) = 1,279$.

That is, the total receipts less the expenses should equal the money in the cash tin. For every credit there must be a debit, so the balance of £1,279 must be entered on both sides of the ledger.

Dr.			Cash Account		Cr.
April 1	Capital	1,000	April 5	Purchases	600
April 8	Sales	430	April 15	Advertising	1
April 17	Sales	450	April 19	Balance c/d	1,279
	Total	£1,880		Total	£1,880

April 19 Balance b/d 1,279

'c/d' is short for carried down, meaning carried into the next trading period. 'b/d' is short for brought down, meaning brought from the last trading period.

(b) Ernie looked at the other accounts:

Capital Account

April 1	Cash	1,000

One figure only, no action.

Purchases account

April 5	Cash	600

One figure only, no action.

Sales Account

April 8	Cash	430
April 17	Cash	450
		£880

Two figures, add.

Expenses Account

April 15	Cash	1

One figure only, no action.

(c) Ernie was then ready to extract the trial balance:

Trial Balance April 19

	Dr.	Cr.
Cash	1,279	
Capital		1,000
Purchases	600	
Sales		880
Expenses	1	
	£1,880	£1,880

The trial balance *did* balance, so he could proceed to his final accounts. The trial balance MUST balance before one can proceed.

3 Location of Errors in the Trial Balance

Go through the following steps in the order in which they are given:
(a) Check the addition of the trial balance.
(b) Check that all the ledger accounts have been included and that they are on the correct side.
(c) Check that the balances have been copied correctly from the ledger.
(d) Look through the entries in the ledger and see if you can spot the difference, e.g.:

Brunel's Trial Balance

	Dr.	Cr.
Totals	£10,000	£10,570

The credits exceed the debits by £570. It is possible that the double entry has not been completed. Look for credit entry of £570 and see whether there is a corresponding debit entry.
(e) Look through the entries in the ledger and see if you can spot half the difference, e.g., using the above example, the credits exceed the debits by £570. It is possible that two credit entries have been made instead of one debit and one credit. Look for a credit entry of £285 and check that the corresponding entry is a debit.
(f) Check the arithmetic in the ledger.
(g) Check the double entry throughout the ledger.
(h) If all else fails, open a suspense account in the ledger.

4 The Suspense Account

So called because one is left in suspense as to the nature of its balance which is held over until a little exploratory work can be done.
Using the example given in 3 (d) above, a debit of £570 is required.

Suspense Account

Trial Balance 570

This can now be added into the trial balance.

	Dr.	Cr.
Totals	10,000	10,570
Suspense	570	
	£10,570	£10,570

Brunel can proceed with his final accounts.

However, this is just a form of 'fiddling'; it is a temporary convenience but matters cannot be left there. So later Brunel asked his friend Archie, an accounting student, to look at his books. Archie found the following mistakes:

(a)   A receipt of £105 was entered in the cash book but included in the Sales account as £501

(b)   There was an addition error in the purchases account, which was undercast by £200.

(c)   A refund of £26 from the local newspaper, for an advertising bill which had been paid twice, was entered in the cash book but nowhere else.

He then corrected them:

(a)   The amount in the sales account must be reduced by 501 − 105 = 396. The balance in the sales account is a credit; to reduce this a debit entry of £396 is made and the credit entry is made in the suspense account.

(b)   The balance in the purchase account is increased by a debit entry of £200: the credit entry is made in the suspense account.

(c)   The refund for advertising reduced Brunel's expenses. So the expense account was credited with £26 and the suspense account debited. Archie completed his work and ruled off the suspense account.

Dr.		Suspense Account		Cr.
Trial balance	570	Sales; figure transposed		
Expenses refund entered in		should be 105	396	
cash book only.	26	Purchases, error in addition.	200	
	£596		£596	

5   Limitations of the Trial Balance

Certain types of error are not revealed by the trial balance:

(a)   Error of principle
Where an entry has been made in the wrong class of account. For instance the purchase of goods for resale may be debited in error to the expenses account instead of to the purchases account.

(b)   Error of commission
Where an entry has been made in the wrong account of the right class of accounts. For example, a charge for rent may be placed in the account of A. Rackham instead of the account of A. Rackman. Accounts for debtors and creditors are discussed in chapter 7.

(c)   Error of omission
This means that the entry has been left out entirely.

(d)   Error in original entry
This is where a mistake is made in copying from the source document which is posted to both sides of the ledger. For example, a receipt of £705 is debited in the

cash book as £507 and posted to the sales account from there.

(e)   Compensating error

This is where a combination of errors cancel each other out—which is not as uncommon as may be supposed. For instance, there can be a complete reversal of the double entry e.g. if a refund is received from an advertising company the entries should be:

Debit cash   credit expenses.

If the opposite is done the accounts will still balance.

Of these errors, the error of principle is probably the most serious as it can alter the accounts substantially and yet be difficult to locate. It is fair to say that it is errors of this type which rock the accounting world and cause firms of auditors to pay heavy compensation.

Errors of omission may be extremely difficult to locate but on a large scale are usually more indicative of fraud than bad book-keeping. Methods of locating all these types of errors are discussed in later chapters.

6   Summary

(a)   A trial balance is a check of the arithmetical accuracy of the ledger.

(b)   It is not part of the double entry system.

(c)   Several types of common error are not revealed by the trial balance but it is still a useful tool.

(d)   The trial balance must balance before the final accounts can be prepared.

(e)   To locate errors in the trial balance go through the steps listed under 'Location of errors' above.

(f)   If desperate, open a suspense account.

Questions

5.1   Bertie opened Woosters' Wonderland to sell garden furniture on October 1st with capital of £10,000, an inheritance from his grandfather who made his fortune in the manufacture of sauce. Bertie did not inherit his grandfather's astute mind.

Oct. 1	Purchased 100 garden tables for £1,800.
	Employed a shop assistant, Barbara, at £60 a week.
Oct. 3	Bought 50 sun loungers for £1,500.
Oct. 4	Paid for wine and nibbles for opening party £150.
Oct. 5	Paid Barbara her wages.
	Paid bill for advertising £50.
Oct. 8	Bought a job lot of sun umbrellas from an auction £600.
	Prospective customer wants tables and chairs to put round his indoor swimming pool.
Oct. 9	Bought 12 chairs for £60.
	Paid month's rent £500.
Oct. 11	Sold 3 tables and 12 chairs for £150.
Oct. 12	Paid Barbara her wages.
	Sold one sun lounger to girl with sun lamp for £35.
	Paid advertising costs of £50.

(a)   Write up the ledger and extract a trial balance.
(b)   Do you think Bertie's shop will be a success?
      Give reasons for your answer.

5.2   On September 1st Bessie Buxton commenced to trade with a capital of £3,000. She paid one month's rent on a shop £100, purchased 12 televisions for £200 each, and employed a salesman at £20 a week.

Sept. 2	She opened the shop.
Sept. 5	5 televisions sold for £220 each.
Sept. 8	1 television sold for £240.
Sept. 10	2 televisions sold for £240 each.
Sept. 11	Paid advertising expenses £20. Took £20 from the till for housekeeping.
Sept. 12	Bought 6 televisions for £1,200.
	Paid salesman's wages.
Sept. 15	1 television sold for £250.
Sept. 16	2 televisions sold for £240.
Sept. 19	Paid salesman's wages.
	Took £20 from the till.
Sept. 23	2 televisions sold for £230 each.
Sept. 25	Paid salesman's wages.
	Took £10 from the till.

Sept. 28   Sold 1 television for £250.
Sept. 30   Paid 1 month's electricity bill of £15.
Write up the ledger and extract a trial balance.

5.3   Give one example of each of the following kinds of error. State whether they will cause the trial balance to disagree, giving reasons for your answer.
    (a)   Error of principle.
    (b)   Error in original entry.
    (c)   The transposition of a number in the credit entry only.

5.4   The trial balance of Knott & Good failed to balance. The debit side exceeded the credit by £330. State what steps you would take in order to locate the error. What would you do if you were unable to make the trial balance agree?

5.5   The trial balance of I.N. Competent failed to agree because the debit exceeded the credit side by £250. This amount was entered in the suspense account. Subsequently the following errors were discovered and corrected:
    (a)   An amount received from sales was credited to the sales account as £102 instead of £201.
    (b)   An amount for cash sales £31 was entered in the sales account but omitted from the cash book.
    (c)   Purchases were overstated by £182.
Write up and rule off the suspense account in the ledger.

Chapter 6 THE TRADING AND PROFIT AND LOSS ACCOUNT

1(a) Definition

The trading account shows the gross profit, that is the profit before the deduction of expenses, while the profit and loss account shows the net profit or loss of the business. These two accounts are known as revenue accounts.

1(b) Explanation

The trading account looks at the difference between the sales and cost of goods sold. This difference is called the gross profit. The gross profit figure can be used in several ways, for example to compare the performance of one business with another and to help in decisions with the pricing of goods for sale.

The profit and loss account takes the gross profit, adds in any non-trading income, and subtracts all the expenses of running the business to find the net profit. This is the real profit of the business before tax. A comparison between the gross and net profit can show if the expenses are reasonable in relation to the size of the business.

2 Book-keeping

As Ernie Enterprise has balanced his trial balance he can proceed to his final accounts. The trading and profit and loss account are part of the double entry system. Ernie must transfer the relevant balances from his ledger to the final accounts.

First he closes the ledger accounts:

Dr.		Purchases Account			Cr.
April 5	Cash	600	April 19	Trading a/c	600

		Sales Account			
April 19	Trading a/c	880	April 8	Cash	430
			April 17	Cash	450
		£880			£880

		Expenses Account			
April 15	Cash	1	April 19	P and L a/c	1

Then he opens his trading and profit and loss accounts:

Trading Account April 19

Purchases	600	Sales	880
Gross profit	280		
	£880		£880

Profit and Loss Account April 19

Expenses	1	Gross profit	280
Net profit	279		
	280		280

He has made a profit of £279. This belongs to him so he places it in his capital account, and then balances it.

Capital Account

April 19	Balance c/d	1,279	April 1	Cash	1,000
			April 19	Net profit	279
		£1,279			£1,279
			April 19	Balance b/d	1,279

He has completed the double entry for all the transactions which are summarised below:

Dr.	Cr.	Amount
Trading	Purchases	600
Sales	Trading	880
P and L	Expenses	1
Trading	P and L	280
P and L	Capital	279

2(a)   Closing Stock

Flushed with success, Ernie bought four cars for £1,260 on April 21.

April 21   Bought paint to respray rusty bodywork £60.
April 22   Sold one car for £420.
April 24   Sold one car for £460.
April 26   Paid for advertising £25.
            Sold one car for £480.
April 27   Wrote up his ledger which he had neglected while working on his cars. Extracted a trial balance and then calculated his gross and net profit for the week.

Cash Account

April 19	Balance b/d	1,279	April 21	Purchases	1,260
April 22	Sales	420	April 21	Purchases	60
April 24	Sales	460	April 25	Expenses	25
April 26	Sales	480	April 26	Balance	1,294
		£2,639		c/d	£2,639
April 26	Balance b/d	1,294			

Capital Account

			April 19	Balance b/d	1,279

Purchases Account

April 21	Cash	1,260
	Cash	60
		£1,320

Sales Account

			April 22	Cash	420
			April 24	Cash	460
			April 26	Cash	480
					£1,360

Expenses Account

April 25	Cash	25

Trial Balance April 26

	Dr.	Cr.
Cash	1,294	
Capital		1,279
Purchases	1,320	
Sales		1,360
Expenses	25	
	£2,639	£2,639

Two points must be noted:
(i)   The paint to respray the rusty bodywork is used to improve the condition of the cars and increase their value. It is included in purchases rather than in expenses, as it is resold, though on the vehicles rather than in the tin.
(ii)   Ernie has bought four cars but only sold three. In order to prepare his final accounts he must place a value on the remaining car. The normal method for valuing stock is the lower of cost and net realisable value. Ernie is selling his cars at a profit, so cost must be the lower value. Four cars cost £1,260 plus the paint at £60, total £1,320. Therefore one car costs

$$\frac{1,320}{4} = 430.$$

Ernie wants to show his one remaining car in his accounts; after all he has paid for it and it is an asset. Therefore, he opens a new account and calls it stock.

Stock Account

April 26   Stock-on-hand   430

For every debit there must be a credit. The credit goes directly into the trading account. However, this is a peculiar credit; it goes on the debit side in brackets and is subtracted from the purchases. This is more sensible than may appear at first sight. The trading account is concerned with the difference between the value of sales and the cost of sales.

Purchases − stock-on-hand = cost of sales.
1,320   − 430   = 890

Trading Account April 26

Purchases	1,320	Sales	1,360
Less stock-on-hand	(430)		
Cost of sales	890		
Gross profit	470		
	£1,360		£1,360

Profit and loss account April 26

Expenses	25	Gross profit	470
Net profit	445		
	£470		£470

Ernie completes his double entry and rules off his ledger.

Purchases account

April 21	Cash	1,260			
	Cash	60	April 26	Trading a/c	1,320
		£1,320			£1,320

Sales account

			April 22	Cash	420
			April 24	Cash	460
April 26	Trading a/c	1,360	April 26	Cash	. 480
		£1,360			£1,360

Expenses account

April 25	Cash	25	April 26	P and L a/c	25

Capital account

			April 19	Balance b/d	1,279
April 26	Balance c/d	1,724	April 26	Net Profit	445
		£1,724			£1,724
			April 26	Balance b/d	£1,724

2(b) Opening Stock

Ernie continued his business for a further week.

April 29   Bought four cars for 1,170
May 1   Sold three cars for £1,320
May 3   Paid advertising £25.
May 4   Valued his two remaining cars at cost £590. Wrote up his ledger, extracted a trial balance and prepared his weekly accounts.

The working of the stock account is shown in detail below.

(i)   The stock account as shown at April 26

Stock account

April 26	Stock-on-hand	430

This was the stock at the beginning of week ending May 3. This stock at start must be included in the trading account. So Ernie credits the stock account and debits the trading account.

Stock account

April 26	Stock-on-hand	430	May 3	Trading a/c	430

Trading account May 3

Stock at start	430	Sales	1,320
Purchases	1,170		

(ii)   The stock on May 3 was valued at £590. So the stock account is debited with the value of stock-on-hand and the trading account credited.

Stock account

April 26	Stock-on-hand	430	May 3	Trading a/c	430
May 3	Stock-on-hand	590			

Trading account May 3

	£		£
Stock at start	430	Sales	1,320
Purchases	1,170		
Stock-on-hand	(590)		
Cost of sales	1,010		
Gross profit	310		
	£1,320		£1,320

Profit and loss account May 3

Expenses	25	Gross profit	310
Net profit	285		
	£310		£310

The Cash and Capital accounts in Ernie's ledger are shown below; the remaining accounts have been omitted.

Cash account

April 26	Balance b/d	1,294	April 29	Purchases	1,170
May 1	Sales	1,320	May 3	Expenses	25
			May 3	Balance c/d	1,419
		£2,614			£2,614
May 3	Balance b/d	£1,419			

Capital account

			April 26	Balance b/d	1,724
May 3	Balance c/d	2,009	May 3	Net Profit	285
		£2,009			£2,009
			May 3	Balance b/d	£2,009

3   Valuation of Stock

The accuracy of the valuation placed on stock is crucial to the results shown in the final accounts. If the stock valuation is too high profit is inflated, if too low profit is depressed. This fact can be used by unscrupulous business men who may fraudulently manipulate their accounts for tax or other reasons. However, there are certain difficulties in placing a valuation on stock. Normally, in questions set in examinations a valuation will be given for closing stock. Nevertheless, it is necessary to understand the common methods of stock valuation.

3(a)   Stocktake

In order to value it is essential to know the type and quantity and condition of the stock-on-hand. This is usually done by means of an annual stocktake. Some stock may be damaged, obsolete or worthless and must be valued accordingly.

3(b) Valuation

Stock should be valued at the lower of cost and net realisable value.

If the price has gone down: value at the new price. If the price has risen: value at cost.

Even in times of inflation prices, more particularly prices of raw materials, can fall and it would be unsound to take the profit before the goods were actually sold.

There are several methods of arriving at 'cost price' and the more common of these are outlined below. Different methods may give substantially different results and it is most important that whatever method is chosen it is used consistently.

(a) F.I.F.O. (First in first out)

This is the method most commonly used. The presumption is that the oldest merchandise is sold first.

This is necessarily true in the case of perishable goods. The calculation is shown by the following illustration:

A. Company has stock on hand of 900 widgets at December 31.

The purchases during the previous three months are shown below.

		No. of units	Cost	Value
Stock-on-hand	Sept. 30	700	—	£350
	Oct.	600	60p	£360
Purchases	Nov.	800	70p	£560
	Dec.	500	80p	£400
		2,600		£1,670

The 900 widgets on hand at December 31 are valued from the most recent invoices:

Dec.	500	80p	£400
Nov.	400	70p	£280
	900		£680

The popularity of this method is due to:

(i) The ease of calculation.

(ii) The lack of requirement to keep a continuous record of purchases and sales.

(iii) The realistic valuation of stock at current prices keeping profits looking healthy.

The drawback of this method is that in times of inflation profit tends to be overstated.

(b) L.I.F.O. (Last in first out)

This method is rarely used; it is the opposite of the FIFO method. Using the above example, the 900 widgets on hand at December 31 are valued from the oldest stock.

Stock	Sept. 30	700	—	£350
	Oct.	200	60p	£120
		900		£470

The advantage of this method is that the cost of sales is shown at a figure which approximates to current prices and that profit is not artificially inflated.

The disadvantages of this method are that:

(i) The stock on hand is shown at a value which may bear no relationship to current prices.

(ii) Several different valuations may be given on the same information, depending on the details given for sales.

LIFO is only recommended in special circumstances by the Institute of Chartered Accountants in England and Wales but is in use in other countries throughout the world.

(c) Average cost

The value of the stock brought forward from the previous period is averaged with the purchases during the period. Using the above example, the 900 widgets on hand at December 31 are valued at

$$900 \times \frac{£1,670}{2,600} = £578 \cdot 08$$

The advantage of this method is that: It is a compromise between FIFO and LIFO and will average out fluctuations in price which may be considerable on the world commodity markets. The disadvantages of this method are that:

(i)   Stock-on-hand is shown at a value which may bear no relationship to current prices.

(ii) It is necessary to keep detailed records of purchases and perform lengthy calculations.

(iii) Several different valuations may be given on the same facts, depending on the periods for calculating the average.

3(c) The Effect of the Valuation on the Accounts

Using the example given above, sales during the three month period were £1,500.

Trading account December 31

	FIFO	LIFO	Average
Stock Sept. 30	350	350	350
Purchases	1,320	1,320	1,320
Less stock Dec. 31	(680)	(470)	(578)
Cost of sales	990	1,200	1,092
Gross profit	510	300	408
Sales	1,500	1,500	1,500

It must be noted that the effect of the difference in valuation is exaggerated in the above example by giving the stock at September 30 the same valuation in all three cases. The effect will be muted when a consistent basis is used.

4 Summary

(a) The purpose of the trading account is to find the gross profit.
(b) The purpose of the profit and loss account is to find the net profit.
(c) Opening stock: Dr. Trading account
                     Cr. Stock account
(d) Closing stock: Dr. Stock account
                     Cr. Trading account (left side in brackets)
(e) Valuation of stock crucial to accuracy of accounts.
      Three methods of valuation are FIFO, LIFO and Average cost.

Questions

For questions **6.1** and **6.2** enter the transactions in the ledger, extract a trial balance and draw up a trading and profit and loss account at the end of the period.

6.1

June 1	S. Sunbeam began to trade in motor cycles and accessories with a capital of £7,500.
June 2	Bought accessories from wholesaler £2,000.
June 3	Bought six motor cycles £5,000.
June 7	Cash sales £750.
June 8	Sold a motor cycle £1,100.
June 11	Paid rent on premises for the month £150.
June 18	Weekly sales £2,250.
June 21	Paid expenses of £95.
June 22	Purchases of accessories £2,000.
June 25	Weekly sales £2,300.
June 30	Sales £1,300.

Value of stock-on-hand on June 30 £3,200.

6.2 Sunny continued to trade:

July 1	Purchased coffee and biscuits for shop £4.
July 9	Sales £2,950.
July 12	Purchases £6,000.
July 13	Paid rent £150.
July 16	Sales £2,400.
July 23	Expenses £120.
	Paid student for assistance £10.
July 30	Sales £2,500.
	Paid student £10.

Stock-on-hand July 31 £3,400

6.3 From the following trial balance prepare a trading and profit and loss account:

Trial balance August 31 19x5

	Dr. £	Cr. £
Capital		10,000
Cash	10,500	
Sales		42,000
Stock Sept. 1 19x4	7,000	
Purchases	30,000	
Expenses	5,000	
Insurance commission		500
	£52,500	£52,500
Stock-on-hand August 31 19x5 valued on FIFO basis		£8,000

6.4 From the following trial balance prepare a trading and profit and loss account:

Trial balance April 30 19x7

	Dr. £	Cr. £
Capital		5,000
Cash	3,750	
Stock May 1 19x6	2,500	
Sales		11,500
Purchases	7,350	
Sales returns	450	
Rent	1,750	
Expenses	750	
Purchase returns		50
	£16,550	£16,550
Stock-on-hand April 30 19x7 Valued on FIFO basis		£3,000

6.5 Using the facts in question 5.1, calculate the value of Bertie's stock on October 12 at cost price.

Draw up Bertie's trading and profit and loss account for the two weeks to October 12.

6.6 Using the facts in question 5.2, calculate the value of Bessie's stock on September 30 at cost price on a FIFO basis.

Draw up Bessie's trading and profit and loss account for the month to September 30.

6.7   Using the trial balance given in question 6.4, draw up a trading account assuming:
   (a)   Stock-on-hand April 30 19x7 is valued on a LIFO basis at £2,400.
   (b)   Stock-on-hand April 30 19x7 is valued at an average cost of £2,650.
Compare the gross profits obtained by the three different stock valuations and comment on the advantages and disadvantages of each method.

6.8   On August 30 Sunny Sunbeam had the following stock valued at cost price.

6 motor cycles	£900 each
25 spare tyres at	£15 each
50 crash helmets	£50 each

During the month he performed the following transactions:

	Sales	Purchases	Date of Purchases
Motor cycles	6 at £1,200	4 at £925	Aug. 11
	6 at £1,250	4 at £975	Aug. 19
		2 at £950	Aug. 27
Spare tyres	10 at £18 ·	5 at £16	Aug. 24
Crash helmets	25 at £60	—	

   (a)   Calculate the value of Sunny's closing stock showing the method of your valuation.
   (b)   Draw up a trading account for the month.
   (c)   Justify the method you have used to value stock.

6.9   From the following list of balances draw up a trial balance at December 31 19x5, fill in the missing capital and prepare a trading and profit and loss account:

	£
Cash	9,250
Stock Jan. 1 19x5	7,500
Sales	70,000
Purchases	49,000
Expenses	2,250
Rent	7,500
Insurance commission	450
Stock Dec. 31 19x5	8,500

Chapter 7 THE BALANCE SHEET

1(a) Definition

A balance sheet is a statement of the financial position of a business at a given date.

1(b) Explanation

A balance sheet is not part of the double entry system, it is merely a summary of the balances remaining in the ledger after the trading and profit and loss accounts have been prepared. By convention the liabilities (which are credit balances in the ledger) are listed on the left side, and the assets (debit balances) are listed on the right side. This means that balances are listed on the sides opposite to those in the ledger.

2 Book-keeping

Ernie Enterprise considered his books as at May 3 (shown in Chapter 6) and decided to draw up a balance sheet. There were balances in the capital, cash and stock accounts.

Ernie Enterprise

Balance Sheet as at May 3

	£		£
Capital	2,009	Stock	590
		Cash	1,419
	£2,009		£2,009

As the name implies the two sides of the balance sheet must be equal.

3 Debtors and Creditors

On May 6 Michael Forbes offered Ernie £800 for the remaining car but was unable to pay immediately as he would have to sell his own car first. Ernie agreed and recorded the sale in his ledger. He needed to record that M. Forbes owed him

£800, so he opened a new ledger account and headed it M. Forbes. Michael had received a car, so the car is shown coming into his account as a debit; the credit is in the sales account.

Dr.		M. Forbes account			Cr.
May 6	Sales	800			

		Sales account			Cr.
			May 6	M. Forbes	800

On May 14 Michael paid Ernie the money he owed. Money comes in, debit the cash account; Michael's debt is now cancelled, so credit his account.

Dr.		M. Forbes account			Cr.
May 6	Sales	800	May 14	Cash	800

		Cash account	
May 3	Balance b/d	1,419	
May 14	M. Forbes	800	

The principle is the same for goods bought on credit. On May 10 Ernie bought two wrecks from Ronald Ragg, the scrap merchant, for £130 on credit. To record this in his ledger, Ernie opened an account for R. Ragg; R. Ragg had disposed of the cars so his account is credited. The purchase account is debited.

Dr.		R. Ragg account			Cr.
			May 10	Purchases	130

		Purchases account	
May 10	R. Ragg	130	

On May 19, Ernie paid Ronald. The cash account was credited—money going out—and Ronald's account debited, as he received the money.

Dr.		R. Ragg account			Cr.
May 19	Cash	130	May 10	Purchases	130

		Cash account			
May 3	Balance b/d	1,419	May 19	R. Ragg	130
May 14	M. Forbes	800	May 19	Balance c/d	2,089
		2,219			£2,219
May 19	Balance b/d	£2,089			

Debtors and creditors accounts are usually grouped together under their respective headings. Debtors are people who owe money to the business and they have a debit balance on their ledger accounts. Creditors are those to whom the business owes money; they have a credit balance on their ledger accounts. Frequently it is more convenient to separate the debtors and creditors accounts from the rest of the ledger in their own books, set of cards or computer print-out. These are then referred to as the debtors ledger and the creditors ledger. They are still part of the main ledger and the double entry system.

There are two types of creditors: *trade creditors*, from whom stock has been purchased and *expense creditors* from whom goods or services for immediate consumption have been purchased.

A business may have dealings with another firm both as purchaser and as vendor. In this case it is usual to open two ledger accounts for the firm, one in the debtors ledger and the other in the creditors ledger. At the end of the month or whenever payment is due, it is sensible to make a transfer between the accounts to discover the net amount due. For example:

Debtors ledger

X Ltd. account

Nov. 30	Balance b/d	450

Creditors ledger

X Ltd. account

	Nov. 30	Balance b/d	500

The balance in the debtors ledger is the smaller so it is transferred to the creditors ledger and the remaining balance paid to X Ltd.

Debtors ledger

X Ltd. account

			Nov. 30	Transfer to creditors ledger
Nov. 30	Balance b/d	450		450

Creditors ledger

X Ltd. account

Nov. 30	Transfer from debtors ledger	450	Nov. 3	Balance b/d	500
Nov. 30	Cash	50			
		£500			£500

Balances remaining on the debtors and creditors accounts are shown on the balance sheet. The accounts are not listed separately but one total is given for creditors and another for debtors.

4 The Bank Account

Ernie decided that, since he was now trading on credit, he should open a bank account for his business. He had opened a personal account when a student so he already knew the advantages: security, an independent record of transactions, and the possibility of loans and overdraft facilities, not to mention a host of well advertised ancillary services. On May 20 Ernie took £2,000 to his bank and opened a current account. To record this in his ledger he opened a new account called the bank account:

Bank Account

| May 20 | Cash | £2,000 | | | |

Cash account

| May 19 | Balance b/d | 2,089 | May 20 | Bank | £2,000 |

The transactions in the bank account are recorded in the same way as those in the cash account. When cheques are drawn the bank account is credited; when cheques are received and paid into the bank, the bank account is debited.

5 The Balance Sheet

Ernie traded until May 31, when he extracted a trial balance and drew up a trading and profit and loss account. The balances remaining on his ledger are listed below:

	Dr. £	Cr. £
Capital		2,633
Cash	67	
Bank	2,116	
Stock May 31	660	
Debtors		
N. Khan	420	
Creditors		
Universal Tyre Supplies		80
United Car Auctions		550
	£3,263	£3,263

Ernie prepared his balance sheet:

Ernie Enterprise

Balance Sheet as at May 31

	£		£
Capital	2,633	Current Assets	
		Stock	660
		Debtors	420
Current liabilities		Bank	2,116
Creditors	630	Cash	67
	£3,263		£3,263

Current assets are those assets acquired for disposal in the course of trade and which will quickly be renewed. Examples of this are stock, debtors and cash. There is a continuing cycle: stock is sold and is exchanged for debtors who in turn discharge their debt in cash, which is used for the purpose of purchasing further stock. Current assets are usually listed in the order of least liquidity, that is starting with the item most difficult to convert to cash. The accepted order is shown above.

Current liabilities are those liabilities which have to be met within a comparatively short time. Examples of this are creditors, bank overdraft which is repayable on demand, and loans repayable within one year. The balance sheet is a summary of the balances remaining on the ledger after the trading and profit and loss account has been drawn up. It is important to realise that the balance sheet shows the stock at the balance sheet date, not the stock per the trial balance; and the capital after the addition of the profit, or subtraction of the loss, for the period, not the capital per the trial balance.

6   Summary

(a)   A balance sheet is a statement of the financial position of a business at a given date.

(b)   It consists of the balances remaining on the ledger after the trading and profit and loss account has been prepared.

(c)   It is not part of the double entry system.

Questions

7.1   B. T. Oven started a music shop. He employed Johann Sebastian, a German student, as his part-time assistant on a salary of £50 per month. He opened a bank account with his £6,000 capital.

May 2	Purchased goods on credit from Musical Supplies Ltd. £1,500.
May 5	Drew £100 in cash from the bank account for float. Bought stamps £12·50 and coffee £4·50
May 7	Purchased goods on credit from Horns and Pipes £3,000. Sold piano on credit to G. Luck £1,500.
May 11	Received bill for rent from R. Rachman £200.
May 11	Sold guitar on credit to L. Garr £700.
May 21	G. Luck paid his debt by cheque. B.T. paid rent by cheque.
May 25	B.T. paid Musical Supplies Ltd. by cheque.
May 29	Bought goods on credit form Musical Supplies Ltd. £1,600. Paid Johann his salary in cash.
May 30	Banked cash sales for the month £2,900. Paid Horns and Pipes the amount due to them.
May 31	Took stock and valued it at £2,700.

Write up the ledger, extract a trial balance, prepare the trading and profit and loss account and the balance sheet as at May 31. Continue the accounts for a further month.

June 2   Received cheque from L. Garr to clear his account.

June 6   Purchased instruments on credit from Horns and Pipes £2,400.

June 10   Sold trumpet on credit to Jeremiah Clarke £250.

June 14   Paid his account with Musical Supplies Ltd.
            Banked cash sales for the fortnight £1,950.
            Received bill for rent from R. Rachman.

June 16   Bought goods on credit from Musical Supplies Ltd. £1,600.

June 18   Sold an organ on credit to F. List £3,000.
            Transferred £100 from the bank to the cash account.

June 21   Bought goods on credit from Musical Supplies Ltd. £1,400.

June 25   Paid Musical Supplies Ltd. £2,050 by cheque.

June 29   Paid Johann his salary in cash.
            Paid the cleaner £10.

June 30   Banked cash sales £2,100.
            Took stock and valued it at £3,200.

Write up the ledger, extract a trial balance, prepare the trading and profit and loss account for June and a balance sheet as at June 30.

7.2   Wooster's Wonderland continued to trade. On October 16 Bertie had capital of £9,171, stock valued at £3,816 and cash of £5,355.

Oct. 16   Opened bank account with £5,200.

Oct. 18   Purchased goods on credit from The Garden Suppliers £1,264.

Oct. 19   Paid Barbara her wages £60.
            Paid advertising charges in cash £50.

Oct. 20   Sold goods on credit to Mr. Abdullah £3,000.

Oct. 22   Purchased goods in auction held by liquidators of failed garden centre £2,000. Paid by cheque.

Oct. 23   Purchased further equipment on credit from Outdoor Venture Ltd. £1,400.

Oct. 25   Transferred £100 from the bank to the cash account.
            Bought garden houses on credit from The Garden Suppliers £1,600.

Oct. 26   Paid Barbara her wages.
            Received bill for advertising charges from I.C.U. Ltd. £50.

Oct. 29   Paid The Garden Suppliers their first invoice by cheque.
            Delivered a further consignment of goods to the docks for Mr. Abdullah, on credit £1,600.

Oct. 30   Banked cash sales £270.

Oct. 31   Took stock and valued it at £6,800.

Write up Bertie's ledger, extract a trial balance and prepare the trading and profit and loss accounts and the balance sheet as at Oct. 31.

7.3 From the following trial balance prepare a trading and profit and loss account and a balance sheet.

Trial balance August 19x6

	Dr.	Cr.
Capital		12,015
Cash	145	
Bank	9,875	
Stock Sept. 1 19x5	8,760	
Sales		96,000
Purchases	80,000	
Sales returns	525	
Purchase returns		175
Debtors		
R. Reed	5,050	
M. Mull	975	
Creditors		
H. Finance		1,060
L. Lease		125
Rent	1,200	
Wages	2,200	
Sundry expenses	645	
	£109,375	£109,375

Stock on hand at August 31 19x6 was valued at £9,350.

7.4 From the following list of balances prepare a trial balance and insert the missing capital. Then prepare a trading and profit and loss account and a balance sheet as at September 10 19x3.

Cash	235	Debtors	
Bank	8,635	I. O. Yew	1,900
Stock Oct. 1 19x2	7,325	D. Dett	75
Stock Sept 30 19x3	8,190	Creditors	
Sales	108,000	J. Shylock	1,315
Purchases	89,000	Rent	2,000
Sales returns	540	Wages	2,275
Purchase returns	260	Interest paid	560

7.5 (a) Define and differentiate between a balance sheet and a trial balance.
(b) Define current liabilities and current assets. Why is it important to distinguish between long and short term liabilities?

7.6 What are the advantages of having a bank account?

7.7 What are the advantages and disadvantages of trading on credit?

Chapter 8   CAPITAL AND REVENUE EXPENDITURE THE VERTICAL BALANCE SHEET

1(a)   Definitions

Capital Expenditure is expenditure on fixed assets. Fixed assets may be defined as assets of a permanent nature by means of which the business is carried on, and which are held for the purpose of earning income and not for resale; that is, they are used continuously in the process of earning income, e.g. land, buildings, plant, machinery, leases, goodwill, motor vehicles. Revenue Expenditure is expenditure on items for resale and for immediate use, e.g. stock, stationery, rent, electricity.

1(b)   Explanation

(i)   *Fixed assets* are not charged to the profit and loss account in the year of acquisition as they should last for several years and are generally expensive items. If these assets were to be charged to the profit and loss account when purchased the profit would be distorted and it would be more difficult to compare accounts from year to year and business to business. Instead, the balances for these items remain in the ledger and are shown on the balance sheet.

In the majority of cases it is a simple matter to decide which assets should be capitalised using the definition given above, but there are problem areas. When an asset is purchased, not only the actual cost of the asset but also any delivery and installation costs should be capitalised. This is because such costs are necessarily incurred in bringing the asset into operating condition. In the case of the purchase of land, buildings and leases there may well be legal fees and stamp duty which may be capitalised. When plant and machinery is purchased, considerable expenditure may be incurred in installation, for instance, in embedding the asset in concrete, or connecting a water, gas or electricity supply; all this would be capitalised. The purchase of motor vehicles must also be treated with care; the seat belts, number plates and delivery charges should all be capitalised, but the motor tax which is an annual charge and the tank of petrol must be charged to revenue. This will probably require the apportionment of the invoice.

Further difficulty arises when an existing asset is modified or improved, as the opportunity to increase the operating efficiency of an asset is often taken when the asset is inoperative due to malfunction. Expenditure on improvements is capital; expenditure on repairs and renewals is revenue. When a repair also constitutes an improvement on the original asset, some division of cost should be made. A reasonable basis for apportionment is to discover the cost for just repairing the assets, to charge that amount to revenue and to capitalise the remainder. However, this may be difficult in practice, especially if the work is performed by the employees of the business. In this event an arbitrary allocation should be made.

(ii) *Revenue items* have been dealt with in previous chapters. They are charged in the trading and profit and loss accounts, which are also known as revenue accounts. There may be some difficulty if the business deals in goods which are also regarded as fixed assets. For example, a firm may manufacture machines for sale and also make machinery for its own use; in that case the machines for resale are stock items and the machines used in the business are capitalised. Similarly, a garage retailing motor vehicles may also provide its employees with cars; the former will be stock, the latter fixed assets.

(iii) *Materiality*

Although all items which fall within the definition of fixed assets may be capitalised, some of them may be of little value and not worth the book-keeping involved. Examples of this might be cutlery in a canteen, hair-grips in a hairdressing salon, and paper-clips in an office. If the item is not capitalised, it is written off to the profit and loss account. The value at which an item becomes material varies considerably from business to business. Large concerns may ignore amounts which would critically affect a small firm. In some firms all items costing less than a given amount are treated as revenue. Such treatment follows the accounting convention of materiality discussed in Chapter 3.

(iv) *The importance of differentiating between capital and revenue*

If capital items are treated as revenue, the assets of the business will be understated as will the profit. This may put a concern in a weak position when negotiating a loan or a bank overdraft; it is axiomatic that these are obtainable only when it can be shown that they are not required, or at the worst mean that the concern is sold or taken over for a sum lower than its true value.

On the other hand, if revenue items are treated as capital, both assets and profit will be overstated and this may lead to the proprietors drawing too much from the firm and leaving it underfinanced.

2 Book-keeping

(a) Example

Ernie Enterprise felt that his business was well established and approached his bank manager for a loan to enable him to purchase a small garage and workshop. The manager was impressed by Ernie's accounts and his future plans and agreed to a loan of £5,000 repayable in five years. At the same time, Ernie negotiated an overdraft limit of £1,000. On July 14 he completed on the garage for £5,000 with legal fees of £500. He purchased tools for £500 and a van for his own use for £1,500. He recorded the transactions in his ledger.

(i) Bank loan

Dr.   Cr.

Loan account B. Bank Ltd. (repayable July 19x5)

| | | July 14 | Bank | 5,000 |

(ii) Purchase of fixed assets:

Freehold land and buildings account

July 14	Bank (Garage)	5,000
	Bank (Legal Fees)	500
		5,500

Tools account

| July 14 | Bank | 500 |

Motor Vehicle account

| July 14 | Bank (van) | 1,500 |

Bank account

July 14	Loan a/c	5,000	July 14	Wiffle and Waffle (garage)	5,500
			July 14	I. N. Monger (tools)	500
			July 14	B. Baker (van)	1,500

If the assets had been purchased on credit, the asset accounts would have been recorded in the same way and the credit entries made in the accounts of Wiffle and Waffle, the solicitors, and I. N. Monger.

The new assets and liabilities were shown on Ernie's balance sheet as at July 31:

Ernie Enterprise

Balance Sheet as at July 31

	£	£		£	£
Capital		3,220	Fixed assets		
			Freehold premises		5,500
Long-term loans			Tools		500

	£	£			£	£
B. Bank Ltd.		5,000	Motor Vehicles			1,500
						7,500
Current liabilities			Current assets			
			Stock		970	
Creditors	750		Debtors		1,010	
Bank overdraft	626		Cash		116	
		1,376				2,096
		£9,596				£9,596

Fixed assets usually apppear above current assets on the balance sheet and are totalled separately. Like current assets, they are shown in the order of least liquidity, premises generally being sold less frequently than motor vehicles. The accepted order is freehold premises, leasehold premises, plant and machinery, tools, furniture and fittings, office machinery, and motor vehicles.

(b) Asset acquired by firm's own labour

A builder decided to build his own offices and include a small flat for himself. The costs were as follows:

	£
Freehold land	5,000
Legal costs for purchase and planning permission	700
Cost of materials	9,850
Wages of men employed on building work	6,900
Salary of foreman supervising building work	2,000
Administration costs	150

The owner's flat comprised one-quarter of the finished building.

The ledger account is shown below:

Dr.		Freehold Premises account			Cr.
April 1	Bank (land)	5,000	July 31	Drawings	6,150
	Legal costs	700		Balance c/d	18,450
July 31	Transfer —				
	Purchases	9,850			
	Wages	6,900			
	Salaries	2,000			
	Admin. Ex.	150			
		£24,600			£24,600
July 31	Balance b/d	£18,450			

The cost of the land and the legal fees can be charged directly to the account when payment is made. The other costs will have been debited previously to other ledger accounts; the materials to purchases; the wages, salaries, and administration expenses to the accounts of those names. Whenever the accounts are prepared, or when the building is completed, the costs must be transferred to the Freehold Premises account. A detailed record must be kept to enable this to be done. A quarter of the building belongs not to the business but to the owner of the business. Therefore, it can be considered as money he withdraws from the business for his personal use. This is not an expense but a reduction in the capital of the business. It is charged to the Drawings account. At the end of the trading period the balance on this account is debited to the capital account.

3   The Asset Register

In order to keep track of the fixed assets and to ensure that none have been bought, scrapped or stolen without being recorded in the ledger, a special book is kept to record the details of every asset. This is additional to the ledger entries and is a check on their accuracy. Every fixed asset is entered in the register when purchased with such details as from whom purchased and the date, the invoice number, the cost, the registration number, the firm's own identifying number, and a brief description. When an asset is disposed of, that information is also recorded.

There are several advantages in keeping the register:

(a)   It is possible to check physically to ensure that the assets on the register are still with the firm and in working order.

(b)   At the same time it is possible to see whether there are any assets unrecorded.

(c)   The totals for each class of asset on the register can be checked against the balances on the ledger. This can help eliminate the errors mentioned in Chapter 5.

(d)   These checks should deter potential thieves employed by the firm who will realise that the asset will be missed.

(e)   The register can also be used to keep a record of maintenance and to pinpoint defective machines.

4   The Vertical Balance Sheet

The two-sided balance sheet which has been shown previously in this book is rapidly becoming outmoded. Most large firms and many smaller ones now use the vertical presentation shown below. Students are advised to use this presentation when answering questions. It has several advantages enumerated below, not the least of which is that there is more space to set out the figures.

Marie Forbes
Balance Sheet as at December 31 19x2

	£	£
Fixed assets		
Freehold premises		10,000
Plant and Machinery		7,500
Furniture and fittings		1,200
Motor vehicles		5,000
		23,700

	£	£
Current Assets		
Stock	4,400	
Debtors	5,600	
Bank	8,000	
Cash	500	
	18,500	
Less current liabilities		
Creditors	7,500	
Net working capital		11,000
Net value of assets		£34,700
Capital		24,700
Long term loan (B. Bank Ltd.)		10,000
Capital employed		£34,700

The advantage of this presentation is that it clearly shows the relationship between certain figures. Current liabilities are subtracted from current assets to give net working capital, that is, the fund available for the day-to-day running of the business.

Fixed assets can be compared with net working capital and the two are added to give the net value of assets. This is equal to the capital employed.

Capital employed consists of both the proprietor's (or shareholders') capital and any long-term loans. Ratios between the various figures can be used to interpret the accounts. These are discussed in detail in Chapter 23.

5   The Limitations of the Balance Sheet

A balance sheet is a statement of the financial position of a business on a given date. It is used by proprietors, shareholders and investors to help them make investment decisions. It is used by bank managers debating whether to grant a loan or an overdraft. It is used by traders deciding whether to give credit. Yet it cannot tell the whole story. It records only those factors which are measurable in monetary terms. It says nothing about the quality of the management or key personnel. It may be that the leading light of the business suffers from ill-health or is due to retire and that this will affect the profitability of the business. To give a further instance, the lease on a firm's premises may be due to expire and not be renewable on favourable terms, so the business will either have to find new premises or be faced with increased overheads.

At present there is little accounting for social responsibility. One firm may meticulously regard the environment and treat all its own waste products, while another apparently identical firm may discharge noxious waste into the local river incurring only trivial fines. The former will probably have higher overhead costs than the latter. In another case one firm may treat its employees more favourably, giving longer holidays and increased pension rights, while another allows only the basic minimum. This could mean that the former will appear less profitable than the latter. Both these factors might well influence prospective investors, but are unlikely to be revealed in the accounts package.

Furthermore, even the monetary values may be misleading. Few firms account for inflation. Most businesses produce historic cost accounts which contain a mixture of 'old' money and 'new' devalued money. This makes it difficult if not impossible to make valid comparisons between firms.

6   Quick definitions

Net Working Capital equals current assets less current liabilities.
Net Value of Assets equals net working capital plus fixed assets.
Capital Employed is equal to the net value of assets and may consist of both Proprietor's Capital and Loan Capital, that is long-term loans.

7   Summary

(a)   Capital expenditure is expenditure on fixed assets. These assets are shown on the balance sheet.
(b)   Revenue expenditure is expenditure on items for resale and immediate use. This is charged to the trading and profit and loss account.
(c)   The concept of materiality must be considered when deciding whether to capitalise an item.
(d)   It is important to differentiate between capital and revenue items in order to obtain accurate accounts.
(e)   The vertical balance sheet is the modern method of presentation, which allows comparisons to be easily made between important figures.

Questions

8.1   P. Ganesh completed his first year's trading, and extracted the following trial balance on 31 March 19x5. Prepare a trading and profit and loss account for the year and a balance sheet as at 31 March 19x5.

	£	£
Sales		25,000
Purchases	17,000	
Carriage in (on purchases)	350	
Carriage out (on sales)	1,500	
Bank interest		55
Rent	2,400	
Wages	600	
Electricity	205	

	£	£
Fixtures and fittings	850	
Motor vehicles	2,500	
Debtors	1,750	
Creditors		1,600
Bank	2,000	
Drawings	2,500	
Capital introduced		5,000
	£31,655	£31,655

Stock-on-hand valued at £2,000.

8.2 The following trial balance was extracted from the books of A. Mazon on June 30 after her first year of trading. Draw up her trading and profit and loss account to show the first year's profit, and prepare a balance sheet as at 30 June 19x7.

	£	£
Drawings	4,000	
Bank overdraft		2,500
Cash	575	
Rates	750	
Debtors	3,500	
Creditors		4,000
Sales		45,000
Purchases	30,000	
Wages	1,200	
Motor car	6,000	
Sundry expenses	425	
Premises	20,000	
Fixtures and fittings	800	
Loan (repayable 5 years)		10,000
Capital introduced		5,750
	£67,250	£67,250

Stock-on-hand was valued at £2,500.

8.3 Draw up a trading and profit and loss account for the year to 3 September 19x9, and a balance sheet at that date from the following:

U. Achebe

Trial Balance

	£	£
Bank	2,600	
Cash	185	
Carriage in	650	

	£	£
Carriage out	375	
Sales		40,000
Purchases	30,000	
Insurance	225	
Rates	1,050	
Debtors	4,125	
Leasehold premises	25,000	
Ground rent	100	
Motor expenses	1,200	
Creditors		3,610
Salaries	6,000	
Drawings	7,000	
Loan (repayable in 3 years)		15,000
Stock at 1 October 19x8	3,000	
Fixtures and fittings	1,100	
Capital at 1 October 19x8		24,000
	£82,610	£82,610

Stock at 30 September 19x9 was valued at £1,500.

8.4   A. Addisson has extracted the following list of balances from his ledger at 31 December 19x1. Prepare a trading and profit and loss account for him and a balance sheet as at 31 December 19x1.

	£
Sales	80,000
Purchases	50,000
Carriage in	115
Carriage out	885
Bank	8,750
Freehold buildings	35,000
Sundry expenses	660
Creditors	4,500
Debtors	6,340
Motor vehicle	5,500
Motor expenses	750
Stock 1 January 19x1	4,000
Rates	1,750
Insurance	350
Electricity	1,090
Fixtures and fittings	4,910
Loan (repayable in 7 years)	5,000
Capital	39,300
Drawings	5,500
Wages	3,200

Stock at 31 December 19x1 was valued at £4,250.

8.5 Ernie Enterprise prepared his trading and profit and loss account for the period ending 30 April 19x3. He brought along the following list of balances and asked you to draw up his balance sheet as at 30 April 19x3 using the modern vertical presentation.

	£		£
Capital 1 August 19x2	3,220	Motor Vehicle	1,500
Loan B. Bank Ltd.		Motor Supplies	
(repayable in 4 years)	5,000	Ltd.	600 Cr.
Stock 30 April 19x3	2,000	Cash	550
Bank overdraft	750	Tools	700
Premises	5,500	F. Freemantle	400 Dr.
H. Hewitt	800 Dr	Fixtures and fittings	1,600
Drawings	3,000	Net profit	
		(8 months to	
		30.4.19x3)	6,480

8.6 Bertie Wooster valued the stock at Wooster's Wonderland on February 28 19x2 at £6,500. He asked Barbara to list his assets and liabilities, and would like a balance sheet as at 28 February 19x2. He does not know his net worth.

Motor car	6,000
Loan from Aunt Agatha	
(repayable in 10 years)	6,000
Cash	100
Bank	980
Mr. Abdullah debtor	4,600
I.C.U. Ltd. (advertising)	250 Cr.
Garden Suppliers	2,500 Cr.
Outdoor Ventures Ltd.	2,250 Cr.

8.7 Define and distinguish between capital and revenue expenditure. Under two headings, capital and revenue, give examples of expenditure that might be incurred by:

        (a)   a hairdresser
        (b)   a riding stable

8.8 Say whether you would treat the following items as capital or revenue and give your reasons.

   (a)   The cost of materials for building a factory extension.
   (b)   Wages paid to men employed on maintenance.
   (c)   Legal fees paid for suing to recover a bad debt.
   (d)   The cost of waste paper baskets in the offices of a multinational company.

(e)   Office furniture £15,000 purchased by a small furniture retailer.
(f)   Installation of central heating in an office block.
(g)   Replacement tyres for cars of sales representatives.
(h)   The cost of laying a tarmac staff car park in a field previously used for that purpose.

8.9   What are the advantages of using a fixed asset register?

8.10   What are the limitations of the historical cost balance sheet for showing the prospects of a business?

8.11   What are the advantages of presenting the balance sheet in the vertical form?

Chapter 9 DEPRECIATION

1(a) Definition

Depreciation is a measure of the exhaustion of the effective life of a fixed asset owing to use, passage of time, or obsolescence. It may be computed as that part of the cost of the asset which will not be recovered when the asset is finally put out of use.

1(b) Reason

The object of providing for depreciation is to spread the expenditure on a fixed asset over its effective lifetime. If depreciation is not charged the accounts are wrong. Another way to view depreciation is as the cost to the business for the use of an asset in the same way as if the business had hired it. Depreciation may be considered both as a measure of the fall in value of an asset and as a means of spreading or amortising its cost.

2 Explanation

(a) Use

Most fixed assets suffer from wear and tear in use; eventually they will break down and have to be replaced. An obvious example of this is a motor car which rapidly wears out and rusts. Other assets like this are plant and machinery, fixtures and fittings and furniture.

(b) Passage of time

All assets have a finite life and this applies as much to buildings as to motor cars although the former may last considerably longer than the latter. Even if a building is increasing in value owing to a general rise in building costs, it is still steadily deteriorating and a point will be reached when the cost of repairs and maintenance will necessitate a move to a new building. Therefore depreciation must be provided for on buildings. Other types of asset will deteriorate even though unused, for example machines may rust.

(c)   Obsolescence

Obsolescence may be defined as the fact that an item is going out of use owing to new technology and changes in the market. Before an asset has worn out it may be superseded by a more efficient model. When this happens the managers of a business may decide to replace the old asset with the new model in order to remain competitive. A computer is a good example of an asset which sometimes needs replacement in order that a new model may carry out its functions more competitively than the predecessor, and require less space. Another example is the aeroplane which is designed to carry a heavier load further and more economically before refuelling.

On the other hand fashions change, and it may be no longer possible to sell a product which has hitherto been profitable. Any specialised tools or machines for making this product will become obsolete. It may be possible to adapt them to manufacture a new product, or it may be necessary to scrap them.

In practice it is very difficult to decide when an asset is likely to become obsolete.

3   Special Kinds of Assets

LAND

Generally this is not considered to deteriorate and need not be depreciated unless there are special circumstances which require it.

MINES AND QUARRIES

These are known as wasting assets, as over a period of time they will be used up completely. Depreciation should be related to the amount extracted.

LEASES

As these are for a fixed period of time the cost is usually amortised over the life of the lease on a straight-line basis.

4   Technical

To determine the amount of depreciation it is necessary to take into account:
(a)   The original cost of the asset or its most recent valuation.
(b)   Its expected life, taking into account the possibility of obsolescence.
(c)   Its approximate value at the end of its working life, known as the residual value.

It can be difficult to ascertain a realistic residual value for an asset. If the amount is likely to be small in relation to cost, as in the case of scrap, it is convenient to regard this value as 'nil'.

BOOK-KEEPING

To record the depreciation it is necessary to open two new accounts in the ledger:
(a)   Provision for depreciation account (CR balance).
This is a 'negative asset' account and the balance on this is recorded on the balance sheet.
(b)   Depreciation account (DR balance).
This is an expense account and is charged annually to the Profit and Loss account.

It is important to realise that the normal asset accounts (Machinery account, Motor vehicles account etc.) will remain unchanged. Such accounts only alter when an asset is purchased, disposed of or revalued. This method is used in preference to other methods because a company is required to show the cost (or most recent valuation) of an asset together with the accumulated depreciation in the accounts.

There are two main methods of depreciation:

(1)   THE STRAIGHT-LINE METHOD

By this method the loss in value is apportioned in equal instalments over the expected life of the asset and the same amount charged annually to the profit and loss account.

The advantages of this method are:
(a)   Its simplicity; the calculation need only be performed once at the beginning of the asset's life.
(b)   The asset eventually reduces to zero value; if it is still performing a useful function it is a signal to revalue the asset.

The disadvantages of this method are:
(a)   It is possible to make an error and continue to depreciate an asset after it has reached zero value, as the same amount is charged each year.
(b)   It makes no allowance for the fact that assets tend to depreciate more quickly in the early years of their life.

Example
A machine which cost £10,000 is estimated to have a useful life of ten years after which it will be sold for scrap. Show the ledger accounts for the first three years together with the asset entries in the balance sheets.

Workings   Assume residual value nil.
Charge £1,000 per annum to profit and loss account.

Dr.		Machinery Account			Cr.
		£			£
Year 1	Cash	10,000			

Dr.		Provision for Depreciation Machinery Account			Cr.
		£			£
Year 1	Balance c/d	1,000	Year 1	Depreciation A/c	1,000
		£1,000			£1,000
			Year 2	Balance b/d	1,000
Year 2	Balance c/d	2,000	Year 2	Depreciation A/c	1,000
		£2,000			£2,000
			Year 3	Balance b/d	2,000
Year 3	Balance c/d	3,000	Year 3	Depreciation A/c	1,000
		£3,000			£3,000
			Year 4	Balance b/d	3,000

Dr.		Depreciation Account			Cr.
		£			£
Year 1	Prov. for Dep. Machinery A/c	1,000	Year 1	P. & L. A/c.	1,000
		£1,000			£1,000
Year 2	Prov. for Dep. Machinery A/c	1,000	Year 2	P. & L. A/c.	1,000
		£1,000			£1,000
Year 3	Prov. for Dep. Machinery A/c	1,000	Year 3	P. & L. A/c.	1,000
		£1,000			£1,000

Profit and Loss Account

Year 1

Expenses		Gross profit	
Depreciation	1,000		

Year 2

Expenses		Gross profit	
Depreciation	1,000		

Year 3

Expenses		Gross profit	
Depreciation	1,000		

Balance Sheet

    Year 1
        Fixed Assets

	Cost	Dep.	NBV
Machinery	10,000	1,000	9,000

    Year 2
        Fixed Assets

	Cost	Dep.	NBV
Machinery	10,000	2,000	8,000

    Year 3
        Fixed Assets

	Cost	Dep.	NBV
Machinery	10,000	3,000	7,000

(2) THE REDUCING BALANCE METHOD

By this method a fixed rate per cent is written off annually from the net book value of the asset. The net book value or written down value is the cost of the asset less the accumulated depreciation.

The advantage of this method is that it makes allowance for the increased loss in value in the early years of an asset's life and the increasing repairs later on when the profit and loss account might otherwise receive an undue charge.

The disadvantage of this method is that it is more difficult to calculate, both initially in determining the appropriate percentage to use, and in that a new figure for depreciation must be calculated annually.

Example

A machine which cost £10,000 is estimated to have a useful life of ten years after which it will be sold for scrap. Therefore 40 % will be written off annually. Show the relevant ledger accounts for the first three years together with the asset entries in the balance sheets.

Dr.		*Machinery Account*			Cr.
Year 1	Cash	10,000			

Dr.		*Provision for Depreciation Machinery Account*			Cr.
Year 1	Balance c/d	4,000	Year 1	Depreciation A/c	4,000
		£4,000			£4,000
			Year 2	Balance b/d	4,000
Year 2	Balance c/d	6,400	Year 2	Depreciation A/c	2,400
		£6,400			£6,400

			Year 3	Balance b/d	6,400
Year 3	Balance c/d	7,840	Year 3	Depreciation A/c	1,440
		£7,840			£7,840
			Year 4	Balance b/d	7,840

Dr.			*Depreciation Account*		Cr.
Year 1	Prov. for Dep.		Year 1	P. & L. A/c.	4,000
	Machinery A/c	4,000			
		£4,000			£4,000
Year 2	Prov. for Dep.		Year 2	P. & L. A/c.	2,400
	Machinery A/c	2,400			
		£2,400			£2,400
Year 3	Prov. for Dep.		Year 3	P. & L. A/c	1,440
	Machinery A/c	1,440			
		£1,440			£1,440

Profit and Loss Account

Year 1

Expenses		Gross profit
Depreciation	4,000	

Year 2

Expenses		Gross profit
Depreciation	2,400	

Year 3

Expenses		Gross profit
Depreciation	1,440	

Balance Sheet

Year 1

Fixed Assets

	Cost	Dep.	NBV
Machinery	10,000	4,000	6,000

Year 2

Fixed Assets

	Cost	Dep.	NBV
Machinery	10,000	6,400	3,600

Year 3

Fixed Assets

	Cost	Dep.	NBV
Machinery	10,000	7,840	2,160

Workings

Year	NBV Jan. 1	Dep. 40%	NBV Dec. 31
1	10,000	4,000	6,000
2	6,000	2,400	3,600
3	3,600	1,440	2,160

Note

A rate of 40% will leave a residual value of £60 after ten years. A rate of 20% will leave a value of £907 and a rate of 50% £10. It will be seen that a very high amount must be charged in the early years by the reducing balance method compared with the straight-line method. This means that the reducing balance method is more suited to assets which have comparatively short lives and lose value very rapidly.

QUESTION WITH ANSWER

Alpha Company Limited was registered this year. It has purchased a car for £10,000 which it will write off over four years, and some office furniture for £1,000 with an estimated life of ten years. The company wishes to use the straight-line method of depreciation and to depreciate for a full year in the year of acquisition. Show the relevant ledger accounts and the balance sheet for this year.

Dr.		Motor Vehicles Account		Cr.
Year 1	Cash	10,000		

Dr.		Office Furniture Account		Cr.
Year 1	Cash	1,000		

Dr.		Prov. for Dep. Motor Vehicles Account		Cr.
		Year 1	Depreciation a/c	2,500

Dr.		Prov. for Dep. Office Furniture Account		Cr.
		Year 1	Depreciation a/c	100

Dr.	Depreciation Account		Cr.
	Year 1		
Motor Vehicles	2,500	P. & L. A/c.	2,600
Office Furniture	100		
	£2,600		£2,600

Profit and Loss Account

Year 1

Expenses		Gross profit	
Depreciation	2,600		

Balance Sheet Year 1

Fixed Assets

	Cost	Dep.	NBV
Office			
Furniture	1,000	100	900
Motor			
Vehicles	10,000	2,500	7,500
	11,000	2,600	8,400

There is a third method of depreciation used in certain circumstances:

ANNUAL REVALUATION

Certain assets cannot be depreciated by the usual methods as stock is continually being used up and added to. Examples of this are livestock (that is, working animals) and loose tools. In these cases a valuation is made at the year end. The fixed asset is then treated in the same way as stock. The old value is debited and the new value credited to the manufacturing or trading account.

The advantage of this method is that it gives an accurate figure in the accounts.

The disadvantage of this method is that it may result in considerable fluctuations in the depreciation charged each year.

Example

Loose tools were valued as follows:

Year 1   Jan. 1   £2,000

              Dec. 31 £2,250

Year 2   Dec. 31 £2,150

Write up the relevant ledger accounts and show the Balance Sheet entries.

Dr.			*Loose Tools Account*				Cr.
Year 1	Jan. 1	Bal. b/d	2,000	Year 1 Dec. 31	Manu. a/c.		2,000
Year 1	Dec. 31	Valuation	2,250	Year 2 Dec. 31	Manu. a/c.		2,250
Year 2	Dec. 31	Valuation	2,150				

Manufacturing Account

Year 1

Indirect expenses

Depreciation   x

Loose tools   Jan. 1   2,000

              Dec. 31   (2,250)

                        (250)

Year 2

Indirect expenses
Depreciation   x
Loose tools   Jan. 1   2,250
            Dec. 31   (2,150)
                      100

Balance Sheet

Year 1

Fixed Assets
Loose tools at valuation   2,250

Year 2

Fixed Assets
Loose tools at valuation   2,150

JOURNAL ENTRIES

Where an accounting system is not computerised and still retains a journal depreciation entries must be recorded therein. In the above example the entries would be shown as follows:

Journal	Dr.	Cr.
Year 1 Manufacturing a/c	2,000	
Dec. 31 Loose tools a/c		2,000
Being transfer of loose tools at Jan. 1 to manufacturing a/c.		
Year 1 Loose tools a/c	2,250	
Dec. 31 Manufacturing a/c		2,250
Being valuation of loose tools at Dec. 31.		

5   The Effect of Inflation on the Value of Assets

A difficulty arises in the concept of depreciation during a period of high inflation in that an asset may keep or even increase its value in monetary terms over the years. For example, it may be possible to purchase a car for £7,000 now and resell it for £7,000 in three years' time. However, by that time the cost of a new car of the same model will have increased significantly. Moreover, the car will have deteriorated visibly during the three years. Therefore it is still necessary to charge depreciation. Nevertheless, it may be considered sensible to revalue an asset to bring its book value in line with its current value. If this is done it will then be necessary to charge more depreciation than formerly, not less.

Example

A machine cost £10,000 two years ago. It is being depreciated on a straight-line basis over ten years. That is, £1,000 is charged annually to the profit and loss account. The machine appeared in the last balance sheet:

Cost	Dep.	NBV
£10,000	£2,000	£8,000

The management decide to revalue the machine at £12,000. The machine has still an expected life of a further eight years. Therefore £1,500 a year must be charged to depreciation in each of the next eight years.

6   Summary

(a)   Depreciation is the expense of using fixed assets in a business. It may be considered both as the fall in value of the asset and an amortisation of cost.

(b)   Depreciation arises on account of:

   (i)   Wear and tear.

   (ii)   Passage of time.

   (iii)   Obsolescence.

(c)   Depreciation is debited in the profit and loss account and credited to the provision for depreciation account which appears on the balance sheet.

(d)   There are two main methods of depreciation:

   (i)   Straight-line method (equal annual instalments).

   (ii)   Reducing balance method (fixed percentage of reducing net book value charged annually).

Questions

9.1   A business purchased a machine for £12,000. Depreciation is to be charged at 20 per cent p.a. by the reducing balance method. Draw up the relevant ledger accounts to show the depreciation over the first three years together with the balance sheet.

9.2   Last year's balance sheet of A. Company showed the following figures for fixed assets:

	Cost	Dep.	NBV
	£	£	£
Machinery	20,000	4,000	16,000
Motor Vehicles	10,000	2,500	7,500
	30,000	6,500	23,500

Machinery is depreciated over ten years and motor vehicles over four years on a straight-line basis. Open the relevant ledger accounts and show the entries for the next two years, together with the balance sheet.

9.3   Define depreciation. Why must depreciation be charged annually on fixed assets?

9.4   Describe the following methods of depreciation:
   (a)   The straight-line method.
   (b)   The reducing balance method.
State the advantages and disadvantages of both methods.

9.5   What factors must be taken into account in determining the amount of depreciation to be charged?

9.6   A five-year lease is purchased for £25,000. Open the relevant ledger accounts in year 1 and show the balance sheet at the end of year 3.

9.7   A manufacturing concern makes a quantity of its own loose tools. Loose tools were valued at £5,000 at the beginning of the year and at £5,500 at the year end. Show the loose tools account in the ledger and the balance sheet entry at the year end.

9.8   After drawing up the trading and profit and loss account the following balances remain in the books of A. Robin. Produce the balance sheet.

	£
Debtors	4,500
Creditors	5,600
Cash on hand	100
Bank overdraft	1,400
Stock	5,000
Motor vehicles	4,000
Fixtures and fittings	3,000
Loose tools	500
Drawings	2,000
Leasehold premises	10,000
Provision for depreciation: fixtures and fittings	12,000
Provision for depreciation: motor vehicles	2,000
Provision for depreciation: leasehold premises	4,000
Net profit	2,500

9.9 From the following Trial Balance prepare a Trading and Profit and Loss account and a balance sheet:

Trial Balance at April 30th

	Dr.	Cr.
Capital M. Forbes		11,765
Cash at bank	550	
Stock	900	
Debtors and creditors	1,060	1,125
Premises	9,000	
Motor vehicles	5,000	
Wages	1,250	
Purchases and sales	5,000	8,000
Fixtures and fittings	1,200	
Bad debts	25	
Rates and insurance	675	
Provision for depreciation: premises		1,710
Provision for depreciation: motor vehicles		2,000
Provision for depreciation: fixtures and fittings		60
	£24,660	£24,660

Stock at close is £750.

Depreciation is to be charged as follows:

Straight-line basis: motor vehicles written off over five years,

Reducing balance method: premises 10 per cent, fixtures and fittings 5 per cent.

Chapter 10   THE CASH BOOK AND THE PETTY CASH BOOK

1   Explanation

There are more entries in the cash and bank accounts than in the other ledger accounts. Therefore, as a matter of convenience, these accounts are kept in a separate book outside the main body of the ledger. In the case of a computerised cash book, this will be printed out separately from the remainder of the ledger and the same principles will apply. The cash book is an integral part of the double entry system. There are several advantages in having a separate cash book; the ledger will not become unwieldy through a large number of cash entries, the cash position can be easily monitored, and different clerks can work on the cash book and the ledger at the same time. If a system is installed whereby clerks can work on only one section of the ledger, errors and fraud may be prevented or detected. For example, the cashier who records receipts in the cash book should not be allowed to make entries in the debtors ledger; if he can, then he may have considerable scope for fraud. When money is received or payment made the transaction is first recorded in the cash book; from there the other side of the entry is posted to the ledger. The cash book is therefore called a book of prime entry.

2   The Two-Column Cash Book

Transactions in both the cash and bank accounts may be recorded in the cash book by using two columns on both sides. This is illustrated by the following example: the cash and bank accounts are first shown in the ledger before a cash book is introduced, and then side by side in the cash book.

Dr.   *Cash account*   Cr.

		£			£
Aug. 1	Balance b/d	100	Aug. 3	Purchases	65
Aug. 7	Cash sales	550	Aug. 6	Advertising	7
Aug. 14	Cash sales	525	Aug. 12	Postage stamps	8
Aug. 21	Cash sales	430	Aug. 25	Wages	985
Aug. 28	Cash sales	380	Aug. 28	Bank	820
			Aug. 31	Balance c/d	100
		£1,985			£1,985
Sept. 1	Balance b/d	100			

Dr.   *Bank account*   Cr.

		£			£
Aug. 1	Balance b/d	4,725	Aug. 5	Typewriter Hire	250
Aug. 7	M. Keyte	350	Aug. 12	C. White	1,500
Aug. 18	Dividends	225	Aug. 18	J. Menzel	1,770
Aug. 26	T. Vought	160	Aug. 20	Insurance	600
Aug. 28	Cash	820	Aug. 25	Salary	550
			Aug. 31	Balance c/d	1,610
		£6,280			£6,280
Sept. 1	Balance b/d	1,610			

Dr.   *Cash Book*   Cr.

		Cash	Bank			Cash	Bank
Aug. 1	Balance b/d	100	4,725	Aug. 3	Purchases	65	
Aug. 7	M. Keyte		350	Aug. 5	Typewriter Hire		250
	Cash sales	550		Aug. 6	Advertising	7	
Aug. 14	Cash sales	525		Aug. 12	Postage stamps	8	
Aug. 18	Dividends		225		C. White		1,500
Aug. 21	Cash	430		Aug. 18	J. Menzel		1,770
Aug. 26	T. Vought		160	Aug. 20	Insurance		600
Aug. 28	Cash sales	380		Aug. 25	Wages	985	
	Cash ¢		820		Salary		550
				Aug. 28	Bank ¢	820	
				Aug. 31	Balance c/d	100	1,610
		£1,985	£6,280			£1,985	£6,280
Sept. 1	Balance b/d	100	1,610				

It must be remembered that, although the cash and bank accounts appear side by side, they are quite distinct from one another and great care must be taken to enter figures in the correct columns. All the entries will be posted to the appropriate ledger accounts with the exception of the transfers between cash and bank accounts. Here the double entry has already been completed and this is signified by writing 'contra' or '$\mathcal{C}$' beside the entries. It must also be remembered that, once a cash book has been introduced, the cash and bank accounts are no longer kept in the main ledger.

3 Discounts

There are three types of discount, trade, contingent and cash.

(a) *Trade discount*
This is usually given on large purchases by other firms. In this case the invoice is made out for the net amount which is entered in sales and debtors and no further book-keeping is required. The discount will not appear in the ledger.

(b) *Contingent discount*
This discount is contingent upon something specified happening later, for instance a certain level of sales being reached. If the purchaser earns the discount he will be credited with it and the discount allowed account will be debited. Such discounts are sometimes offered by very large concerns.

(c) *Cash discount*
This is given if the customer pays within a specified period of time. The invoice is made out for the full amount but the debtor is entitled to deduct a certain percentage of the bill. This is to encourage debtors to pay early and so avoid expensive reminders and improve the cash flow of the business. Unfortunately, some customers may take the discount whether or not they pay on time and it can prove very difficult to recover the small sums of money outstanding.

4 The Three-Column Cash Book

The cash discounts, both those allowed to debtors and those received from creditors, must be recorded in the ledger. It is convenient to make a note in the cash book of these discounts, as it is at the point of payment that one knows whether the discount is being claimed. An additional column is used to record the discount, but it is for memorandum purposes only, and unlike the cash entries it is not part of the double entry system. From the cash book the discount is posted to both sides of the ledger, to the discount account and to the personal accounts of debtors or creditors.

Example
Joe King, the well-known wholesaler of tricks and toys, warned by his bank manager against overstepping his overdraft limit, tried to improve his cash flow by offering a cash discount of $2\frac{1}{2}\%$ if his customers paid within 14 days. The following transactions occurred in August, and were recorded in his cash book (see p. 100).

Cash Book

Dr.

	Particulars	Discount Allowed	Cash	Bank
Aug. 1	Balance b/d		100	
Aug. 7	S. Sillery	1		39
Aug. 9	Cash Sales		1,100	
Aug. 9	Cash ¢			1,000
Aug. 12	M. Potts	10		390
Aug. 13	Miss Chief	5		195
Aug. 16	Cash sales		1,250	
Aug. 16	Cash ¢			1,200
Aug. 23	Cash sales		1,095	
Aug. 23	Cash ¢			1,000
Aug. 29	F. Phunn	6		234
Aug. 30	Cash sales		1,155	
Aug. 30	Cash ¢			1,130
		£22	4,700	5,188
Sept. 1	Balance b/d		100	3,335

Cr.

	Particulars	Discount Received	Cash	Bank
Aug. 1	Balance b/d			500
Aug. 5	Expenses		25	
Aug. 9	Wages		45	
Aug. 9	Bank ¢		1,000	
Aug. 13	Trixie	25		975
Aug. 16	Advertising			50
Aug. 16	Wages		45	
Aug. 19	Bank ¢		1,200	
Aug. 19	Jester Ltd	2		78
Aug. 20	Stationery		65	
Aug. 23	Wages		45	
Aug. 23	Bank ¢		1,000	
Aug. 26	Rent			250
Aug. 30	Wages		45	
Aug. 30	Bank ¢		1,130	
Aug. 31	Balance c/d		100	3,335
		£27	4,700	5,188

Joe King had bank overdraft of £500 on August 1, so the balance at bank is shown on the credit side.

It must be remembered that the discount columns are just for notes and the totals must be posted to both sides of the ledger. The columns are merely totalled and not balanced. It is unlikely that the amounts for discounts allowed and received will be equal. Two ledger accounts must be opened for these amounts. Discount allowed is treated as an expense and discount received as income in the profit and loss account.

The entries in the discount accounts and examples of the entries in the debtors and creditors accounts are shown below.

Dr.		*Discount allowed account*		Cr.
Aug. 31	Debtors C/B	22		

		Discount received account		
			Aug. 31 Creditors C/B	27

Creditors Ledger

Trixie

Aug. 31	Bank C/B	975	Aug. 1	Balance b/d	1,000
	Discount rec. C/B	25			
		£1,000			£1,000

Debtors Ledger

S. Sillery

Aug. 1	Balance b/d	40	Aug. 31	Bank C/B	39
				Discount all. C/B	1
		£40			£40

F. Phunn

Aug. 17	Sales	240	Aug. 31	Bank C/B	234
Aug. 28	Sales	160		Discount all. C/B	6
				Balance c/d	160
		£400			£400
Sept. 1	Balance b/d	£160			

5   The Petty Cash Book

In a sizable concern it would be inefficient to trouble the cashier every time a small sum was required. To overcome this problem a certain sum may be set aside and called petty cash. This sum will be the amount considered necessary to cover minor expenditure during a week or month. The actual amount will vary considerably from business to business but if it is kept low it can be controlled by a junior employee, known as the petty cashier.

5(a)   The Imprest System

The petty cashier will pay money on receipt of a voucher, which might be an invoice for stationery, or a portion of till roll from a supermarket. If no invoice is available, for example for taxi fares or postage stamps, the petty cashier will write out a voucher and obtain the payee's signature. At any time the money in the cash tin together with the total value of the vouchers should equal the amount of the float. This enables spot checks to be made. At the end of the period the petty cashier will be reimbursed for the total of the vouchers on hand. For example:

	£
Cash at beginning of week	100
Payments	(75)
	25
Cash reimbursed	75
Cash at beginning of next week	100

These payments will be recorded in a petty cash book. This may be analysed so that totals can be posted to the various expense accounts. If the business is registered for VAT (Value Added Tax) the petty cash book will contain a column to record the VAT paid so that it can be reclaimed.

An example of an analysed petty cash book is shown opposite. The headings can be altered to suit the individual firm:

The four expense accounts will be debited with the relevant totals. The VAT will be debited to the VAT account and reclaimed from the Customs and Excise. Further details on the working of the tax are given in Chapter 11. As cash sales should be banked daily and entered directly into the bank account the cash book will contain only bank transactions. This leaves sufficient space for analysis columns in the cash book, which can be useful in preventing and checking on errors. Such an analysed cash book might contain the following headings. The actual headings will depend on the information required by the business:

Dr.   *Cr.*

Receipts					Payments				
Discount Allowed	Debtors	Cash Sales	Misc.	Total	Discount Received	Cred-itors	Cash Purchs.	Misc.	Total

The discounts are not included in the 'Total' columns as these relate to monies actually going in and out of the bank account.

6   Refunds and Returned Cheques

(a)   When goods are returned and a cash refund is made, this must be entered in the cash book; it is not correct to deduct the money from cash sales.

(b)   When cheques are returned by the bank marked 'refer to drawer' a credit

Petty Cash Book

Receipts £	Ref.	Date	Details	V.no.	Total £	VAT £	Travelling £	Stationery £	Cleaning £	Misc. £
100	C/B	Aug. 1	Cash	—						
			Stationery	53	11.50	1.50		10.00		
			T. Geary	54	7.00		7.00			
			P. Hulme	55	7.30	.30	5.00			2.00
		Aug. 2	Sundry	56	5.75	.75				5.00
		Aug. 3	K. Rand	57	7.00	.50	1.00			5.50
			F. Heydon	58	8.00		8.00			
		Aug. 4	Stationery	59	10.35	1.35		9.00		
		Aug. 5	M. Mopp	60	12.00				12.00	
			M. Ames	61	6.10	.75	5.35			
			TOTALS		75.00	5.15	26.35	19.00	12.00	12.50
			Balance c/d		25.00					
					£100.00					
75	C/B	Aug. 6	Balance b/d Cash							

£100
25
75

103

entry must be made in the cash book referenced 'contra' or '*¢*'. This will also be placed against the original entry. For example:

Cash Book

		Bank						*Bank*
May 1	T. Twister	£150 ¢	May 22	T. Twister (ret.)	¢			£150

Both entries will be posted to T. Twister's account in the ledger. On no account is the cashier allowed to cross out an entry in the cash book once a cheque has been received or drawn.

When a three-column cash book is in use and discount has been allowed on a returned cheque, a reversing entry must be made in the 'discount allowed' column. If the entry were to be made in the 'discount received' column both discounts would be incorrect. This means that two entries must be made in the cash book for every returned cheque on which discount has been allowed.

Cash Book

		Discount Allowed	*Bank*			*Discount Received*	*Bank*
May 1	T. Twister ¢	3	147	May 22	T. Twister ¢		147
May 22	T. Twister ¢	(3)	—				

Only the relevant columns and entries are shown above.

7 Summary

(a) For convenience and for safety the cash and bank accounts are kept apart from the main body of the ledger in cash books.

(b) A two-column cash book records the cash and bank accounts side by side.

(c) A three-column cash book uses the extra column for recording cash discounts allowed (to debtors) and received (from creditors). This is for memo only and is not part of the double entry system.

(d) Minor cash expenditure is covered by a float which is recorded in the petty cash book.

Questions

10.1 Orson Kart had a rag and bone trade; his cash transactions during February are shown below. You are required to write up a two-column cash book to record these and to bring down the balances at the end of the month.

19X0

Feb. 1	Cash on hand £545, cash at bank £9,876.
Feb. 3	Bought scrap metal for cash £75.
Feb. 5	Paid Steptoe and Son by cheque £465.
Feb. 6	Paid for advertising in cash £8.
Feb. 7	Received cheque from Inland Revenue for tax overpaid £150.

Cash sales £225.
Feb. 12   Purchased hay for horse £25 cash.
          Gave G. Gaffer cheque for £1,500.
Feb. 14   Cash sales £345.
Feb. 18   Banked winnings from the races £240.
          Paid cheque to Abdul Khaliq £1,820.
Feb. 20   Paid insurance premium by cheque £40.
Feb. 21   Cash sales £170.
Feb. 25   Wages paid to schoolboy who grooms the horse £20.
          Orson gives cash to wife for housekeeping £100.
Feb. 26   Banked cheque from Jack Jones £170.
Feb. 28   Cash sales £330. Banked cash of £1,000.

10.2   I. N. Competent asked you to write up his two-column cash book for the month of March. He brought the following list of transactions, 19x2 :

March 1   Cash on hand £50. Bank overdraft £500.
March 2   Bought stationery for cash £10.
March 3   Paid A. Webb £55 by cheque.
March 5   Paid advertising charges in cash £5.
March 6   Paid part-time assistant Val £25.
March 9   Drew cash for business from bank £40.
March 10 Found missing cash from sales and banked it £1,100.
March 11 Paid motor expenses by cheque £120.
March 13 Paid Val £25 cash.
          Drew cash from bank for personal use £150.
March 16 Received cheque £540 from J. Batt.
March 17 Paid pools winnings into bank £75.
March 19 Drew cheque in favour of P. Duane £640.
          Bought coffee for office use £5.
March 20 Paid Val £25.
          Cash sales £740.
March 23 Customer returned goods, gave her £35 cash.
March 24 Claimed car expenses in cash £45.
March 25 Cheque arrived from A. Edge £680.
March 27 Cash sales £830
          Paid Val £25.
          Paid wife housekeeping out of office funds £120.
March 30 Paid cash into bank account £1,250.
Bring down the balances at the beginning of April.

10.3   From the following information write up a three-column cash book and bring down the balances at the end of the month. Post the totals of the discount columns to the relevant ledger accounts.

19x4

April 1	Balances brought down Cash £75, Bank £1,050.
	Expenses for office party paid cash £55.
April 2	Cash sales banked £880.
April 5	Paid A. Edge £490 by cheque taking a discount of £10.
April 6	Received cheque from J. Hall £468, allowed discount of £12.
	Paid for newspaper advertising in cash £15.
	Drew £95 from the bank for office use.
April 8	Paid telephone bill by cheque £65.
April 9	Banked cash sales £920.
	Paid cleaner £25 in cash.
April 12	Received cheque £39 from C. Keay, allowed discount of 2½%.
April 13	E. Lewis paid cheque £78, allowed discount of £2.
	Paid window cleaner £10 cash.
April 14	Cash purchases £55.
April 16	Cash Sales £960. Banked £870.
	Drew cheque for personal use £250.
April 19	Drew cheque in favour of G. Grant £882, received discount of £18.
April 21	Received cheque in settlement of a debt of £360 from E. Long £351, allowed the discount.
April 23	Banked cash sales £840.
	Paid cleaner £25 cash.
April 26	Paid £35 by cheque for motor expenses.
April 30	Cash sales £760.

10.4 W. Wood owns a carpentry business. From the following information write up his three-column cash book for the month of May, bring down the cash balances and post the discount totals to the ledger:

19x6

May 1	Balances brought down Cash £150, Bank £500.
May 2	Cash purchase £100.
May 3	Paid rent by cheque £250.
May 4	Received cheque from B. Bench £388, allowed discount of £12.
May 5	Took £50 cash for personal use.
May 8	Drew cash from bank for office use £150.
	Arranged overdraft facilities with his bank manager.
May 9	Paid E. Oak £975 and received discount of £25.
May 11	Received cheque from T. Table £427 in full settlement of a debt of £440.
May 12	Took £50 cash for personal use.
	Paid telephone bill £56 by cheque.
May 15	Bought stationery £10, stamps £5, and coffee for office use £4 in cash.
May 16	Received cheque from T. Chest £78 allowed discount of 2½%.

May 17   Received cheque from K. Board £975 did not allow discount as a month overdue.

May 19   Took £50 cash for personal use.

May 22   Cheque from K. Board returned marked 'refer to drawer'.

May 24   Dividends received £155.

May 26   Cash sales £700. Banked £580.

10.5   From the following information write up an analysed petty cash book: give analysis columns for stationery, travel, postage, and miscellaneous. The business is registered for VAT. Bring down the balance at the end of the week and restore the imprest to £60. Number the vouchers consecutively.

19x8

June 1   Balance brought down £60. Stationery £3·45 including VAT 45p. Photocopying £2·30 including VAT 30p.

June 2   Postage stamps £2. D. Sales total expenses £9·50: comprising VAT £1·30, travel £7·50 and sundry 70p. Office flowers £4·60 including VAT 60p.

June 3   Newspaper advertising £1·50. R. Vend travel expenses £2·50.

June 4   Replenishment of office first aid kit £8. 'Get well' card for sick colleague 23p including VAT 3p. Donation to charity £5.

June 5   Mrs. Mopp the cleaner £7. Government publication for office reference £2·95. S. Repp motor expenses £7·50 including VAT £1.

10.6   From the following information write up a petty cash book. Give analysis columns for transport, cleaning, stationery and miscellaneous. The business is registered for VAT. Bring down the balance at the end of the week and restore the imprest. Number the vouchers consecutively starting at 57.

19x1

July 23   Balance brought down £100. A. White claimed expenses: travel £5·50, and dinner on train £5·00 plus VAT 75p. Sherry for farewell drink with retiring colleague £11·50 including VAT £1·50.

July 24   Biscuits, coffee and sugar for office use £6. Postage stamps £4. Window cleaner £7·50. Paper and envelopes £4·60 including VAT at 15%.

July 25   B. Black expenses £10·50 including VAT £1·25. Duplicating ink £3·45 including VAT at 15%.

July 26   J. M. Blue expenses: Train fare £6·50, meal £5·75 including VAT at 15%, incidental 50p. R. Redd parking fine £5.

July 27   Paid office cleaner £5, subscription to trade magazine £8, and V. Violet £2·30 for light bulbs including VAT of 30p.

10.7   What is the difference between a cash discount and a trade discount?

10.8   State what you think to be the advantages and disadvantages of offering a cash discount.

Chapter 11   THE SUBSIDIARY BOOKS: PURCHASE, SALES AND RETURNS DAY BOOKS

1   Explanation

As a business expands so does the number of its sales and purchases, and the number of entries in the ledger. The cash book and the debtors and creditors have already been separated from the main body of the ledger. To prevent a complete fragmentation of this and to enable a detailed analysis to be made of sales and purchases, a different system is used for these. They are listed in the sales and purchase day books or journals. These are not part of the double entry system but only subsidiary books; from them individual entries are made to the personal and expense accounts, and total entries to the sales and purchases accounts. If the firm is registered for VAT it is convenient to record the VAT charged to customers (outputs), and the VAT charged by suppliers (inputs) in the day books.

Entries are made directly from invoices. An example of an invoice is shown opposite.

2   The Sales Day Book

In the case of sales, the invoices should be pre-numbered, used chronologically, and entered in numerical order. If an invoice is mutilated the number should still be entered and marked 'void'. The purpose is to ensure that no sales invoices are overlooked in error, and that no employee can raise a sales invoice on his own behalf and be paid directly by the customer. This feature is most important in businesses where sales representatives can collect debts. Entries in the day book are made from copy sales invoices which are then filed in numerical order. These can be used for reference in dealing with customers' complaints, in audit work and in verifying VAT returns. Only credit sales are entered in the sales day book.

The illustration opposite shows a sales day book in its simplest form, suitable for a firm registered for VAT and dealing in goods suffering only one rate of VAT.

Illustration of an Invoice

A. Wholesaler
Trading Estate
Newtown
VAT Registration No. 123 4567 89
Account No. 77
Order No. 559

Invoice No. 2963
Date: 1 April 19x4

To B. Wooster
Woosters Wonderland
Newtown

Quantity	Description	Unit cost £	Total cost £	VAT rate
50	Garden chairs	12	600	20%
12	Garden tables	20	240	
12	Umbrellas	15	180	
			1,020	
	Delivery charges		20	
	Total goods		1,040	
	Total VAT		208	
	Total due		£1,248	

Sales Day Book
Page 5

Date 19x4	Customer	Inv. No.	Acc. No.	Total £	VAT £	Sales £
April 1	B. Wooster	2963	77	1,248	208	1,040
	E. Enterprise	2964	15	1,176	196	980
April 2	B. Brunel	2965	8	432	72	360
April 3	B. Buxton	2966	10	600	100	500
April 4	S. Sunbeam	2967	59	264	44	220
April 5	O. Kart	2968	46	840	140	700
	VOID	2969	—	—	—	—
	E. Enterprise	2970	15	120	20	100
				4,680	780	3,900

At the end of the week, or other specified period, the sales day book is totalled and posted to the ledger, the individual invoices are debited to the debtors accounts, and the total net sales and VAT credited to their respective ledger accounts.

Debtors Ledger

		B. Brunel	*Acc. No. 8*
April 2	SDB 5	432	

		B. Buxton	*Acc. No. 10*
April 3	SDB 5	600	

		E. Enterprise	*Acc. No. 15*
April 1	SDB 5	1,176	
April 5	SDB 5	120	

		O. Kart	*Acc. No. 46*
April 5	SDB 5	860	

		S. Sunbeam	*Acc. No. 59*
April 4	SDB 5	264	

		B. Wooster	*Acc. No. 77*
April 1	SDB 5	1,248	

Sales account

	April 5	SDB 5	3900

VAT account

	April 5	SDB 5	780

3   The Purchase Day Book

Purchase invoices are numbered according to the supplier's system. In order to keep a record of invoices received and to ensure that none are unwittingly mislaid, they should be stamped with a revolving number stamp. This gives them numerical sequence. In large concerns they may also be marked with a box stamp which will be initialled in the appropriate place when it has been checked that the goods were ordered and have been received in good condition and that the invoice is approved for payment. Thus:

No.
Date Ordered
Goods Received
Payment Approved

When a cheque is finally drawn the invoice will be stamped 'paid', marked off in the day book, and filed in numerical sequence. This system can be adapted to suit the needs of different firms, but tight control over the payment of invoices is advisable. There have been frauds whereby firms have been induced into paying high prices for stationery which was neither desired nor required.

An example of a simple purchase day book is given below. Goods are usually packed with a delivery note which is often a duplicate invoice. This should be checked against the goods received, and against the invoice when payment is made. It may be attached to the invoice and filed with it, or filed separately in supplier order. This has the advantage of keeping the duplicate invoices from one supplier together to check against the statement if a query should arise.

Purchase Day Book   *Page 23*

Date	*Supplier*	*Inv. No.*	*Acc. No.*	*Total*	*VAT*	*Purchases*	*Paid*
19x4				£	£	£	
April 1	B. Brock	432	1010	660	110	550	31.5.x4
April 2	E. Emmet	433	1023	6,000	1,000	5,000	31.5.x4
	H. Herr	434	1047	3,000	500	2,500	31.5.x4
April 3	D. Deer	435	1017	1,200	200	1,000	20.5.x4
April 4	E. Emmet	436	1023	900	150	750	20.6.x4
April 5	B. Bumble	437	1012	300	50	250	
				12,060	2,010	10,050	

Postings are made to the individual creditors accounts and to the VAT and purchases accounts.

VAT account

April 5	PDB 23	2,010	April 5	SDB 5		780

Purchases account

April 5	PDB 23	10,050

The paid column gives the date of payment and can be used to explain why payment has not been made, for instance goods not delivered or not ordered. If necessary an appropriate adjustment can be made in the ledger accounts.

4 Analysed Day Books

More detailed information can be recorded by adding further columns as required. For instance, a firm may wish to analyse its sales and purchases by product types. The sales day book might then look like this:

				Sales Day Book					*Page 5*
Date	*Customer*	*Inv. No.*	*Acc. No.*	*Total*	*VAT*	*Chairs*	*Tables*	*Umbrellas*	*Carriage*
				£	£	£	£	£	£
April									
1	B. Wooster	2963	77	1,248	208	600	240	180	20

Several different sales accounts can be opened, for example: sales account (chairs), sales account (tables), and sales account (umbrellas). These can be used to discover market trends and can help management to make policy decisions on which lines to continue to sell, at what price and the quantities to order and keep in stock.

The system can be adapted to cover different departments or sales areas.

Additional columns will be needed if the firm sells goods which bear more than one rate of VAT or which are exempt from VAT.

The purchase day book will contain similar headings and may also include a column for expense items and those which are exempt from VAT.

5 Sales Returns and Purchase Returns Day Books

When goods are returned because they are faulty or unsuitable, a credit note must be raised. It is not sufficient just to cancel the original invoice. There are several reasons for this: the goods returned are not necessarily the only items on the invoice; there is less scope for fraud if the credit notes are pre-numbered and strictly controlled; the list of credit notes shows the reasons for customers' complaints so that the firm has an opportunity to improve its service; finally, if VAT is involved, it is essential to have a credit note, to verify that the tax has been correctly accounted for.

Credit notes are listed in the sales returns day book which has a format similar to that of the sales day book. An example is given below:

				Sales Returns Day Book			*Page 2*
Date	*Customer*	*Cr. No.*	*Acc. No.*	*Total*	*VAT*	*Returns*	*Notes*
April 9	B. Wooster	Cr. 11	77	60	10	50	wrong colour
April 11	E. Enterprise	Cr. 12	15	90	15	75	faulty
April 14	O. Kart	Cr. 13	46	42	7	35	wrong size
				192	32	160	

Individual items are credited to the personal accounts and the totals are debited to the VAT and sales returns accounts. When purchases are returned to suppliers it is good practice to raise a debit note. These are listed in the purchase returns day book, which is set out in the same way as the sales returns day book above, except that there is a debit note number (Dn. No.) instead of a credit note one. When the credit note is received from the supplier it is compared with the debit note and filed with it.

6 VAT Records

This system applies to the United Kingdom; other countries have their own rules on the details necessary for recording their sales tax.

A record must be kept of sales on which VAT has been charged at standard and at any other rate which may be in force. This must include any goods which the proprietor has taken for his personal use. Separate figures must be kept for the VAT actually charged at the different rates. For example, if two rates of VAT, 10 % and 20 %, were in force and half the sales of a certain business comprised goods suffering the lower rate – and half the higher. The firm must show one sales figure excluding VAT (£50,000) and two VAT figures, VAT charged at 10 % on £25,000 (£2,500) and at 20 % on £25,000 (£5,000).

Exports, zero rated sales and exempt sales must be shown as separate figures. It is essential that the sales shown on the VAT returns agree with the figures shown in profit and loss account. The point may seem obvious, but more than one trader has been prosecuted because he failed to take that simple precaution.

Purchases and expenses must be recorded net of VAT. Any exempt items (those on which VAT is not charged) and certain items on which the VAT is not recoverable, must be excluded from the total of purchases and expenses on the VAT return. In order to do this, such items need to be analysed separately. The law covering exempt and non-deductable items is subject to change from time to time. The above figures can be obtained from the analysed day books, the petty cash book, and if necessary a VAT column can be added in the cash book. If this is done, care must be taken to record only the VAT not recorded elsewhere, that is the VAT on cash sales and purchases.

An example of a VAT account for three months appears on p. 114. The reference letters refer to the purchase day book (PDB), the sales returns day book (SRDB), the petty cash book (PCB), the sales day book (SDB), and the purchase returns day book (PRDB). Details of standard and higher rated purchases are not shown as they are not required. The information needed for the VAT return can easily be extracted from the account. The VAT return from 1.4.x4 to 30.6.x4 will be forwarded to the Customs and Excise together with a cheque for £1,900 by 31 July 19x4.

VAT Account

Date	Ref	Standard £	Higher £	Total £		Date	Ref	Standard £	Higher £	Total £
19x4						19x4				
April 30	PDB 23	—	—	1,400		April 30	SDB 6	1,500	500	2,000
	SRDB 2	60	—	60			PRDB 2	—	—	50
	PCB 55	—	—	40		May 31	SDB 9	1,600	400	2,000
May 31	PDB 25	—	10	1,450			PRDB 3	—	—	150
	SRDB 3	40	—	50		June 30	SDB 12	1,850	450	2,300
	PCB 58	—	—	70			PRDB 4	—	—	50
June 30	PDB 27	—	—	1,500						
	SRDB 3	—	30	30						
	PCB 62	—	—	50						
				4,650						
Bal. due to Customs & Excise c/d				1,900						
		100	40	6,550				4,950	1,350	6,550
						July 1	Bal. b/d			1,900

7 Example

Trading Account

Year ended 31 December 19x4

	£	£		£
Stock Jan. 1 19x4		6,000	Sales	106,500
Purchases	73,000		Less returns inwards	(500)
Less returns outwards	(730)			106,000
		72,270		
Less stock Dec. 31 19x4		(7,270)		
Cost of sales		71,000		
Gross profit		35,000		
		£106,000		£106,000

The trading account shows two additional figures, purchase returns (returns outwards) and sales returns (returns inwards). The purchase returns are subtracted from purchases to give net purchases, and the sales returns are subtracted from sales to give net sales. This means that the credit figure for purchase returns appears on the debit side in brackets, in the same way as stock on hand. The debit figure for sales returns appears on the credit side in brackets.

When a business is registered for VAT, the VAT is not shown in the trading and profit and loss accounts; any monies due to or from Customs and Excise appear on the balance sheet.

8 Statements

Many suppliers produce monthly statements which show invoices issued and payments received during the month. These should be reconciled to the creditors ledger account to ensure that no invoices have been omitted and that all payments have been received. This action will help to prevent errors and fraud. However, payments should not be made on statements, but only on invoices. This is to prevent the same bill being paid twice in error.

An example of a statement is shown overleaf.

9 Advantages of Day Books

(a) There can be an increase in office efficiency. If duties are segregated more clerks can work together on the book-keeping.

(b) If duties are carefully segregated, clerks can be in a position to check each other's work, thus providing a good system of internal control and preventing errors and fraud.

(c) There is a complete list of credit purchases and sales. This can be analysed into

Illustration of a Statement

A. Wholesaler
Trading Estate
Newtown
VAT Registration No. 123 4567 89
Account No. 77

STATEMENT
April 19x4

To B. Wooster
Woosters Wonderland
Newtown

Date	Description	Our Ref.	Dr. £	Cr. £	Balance £
March 31	Balance b/f	—	560		560
April 1	Goods	2963	1,248		1,808
April 9	Returns	Cr.11		60	1,748
April 15	Cash	—		560	1,188
April 16	Goods	2998	60		1,248
April 25	Goods	3039	240		1,488
April 30	Cash	—		1,188	300

product groups, sales areas or departments, by weeks, months or any convenient period. This will provide management with the information necessary to make reasonable decisions on manufacture, sales, and marketing. It will also provide the accountants with information on which to base forecasts, budgets and cash flows.

10 Summary

(a) All invoices and credit notes are listed in numerical order in the day books.
(b) There are four day books: purchase, purchase returns (returns outwards), sales, and sales returns (returns inwards).
(c) The day books are books of prime entry. They are not part of the double entry system.
(d) Entries are posted to both sides of the ledger: totals to the sales, purchases and returns accounts; and individual invoices to the personal accounts.
(e) Firms that are registered for VAT record this in the day books, and petty cash book. The balance on the VAT account is money owed to (Cr.) or by (Dr.) Customs and Excise and appears on the balance sheet.

Questions

11.1 Enter the following sales in the sales day book of C. Bird registered for VAT. Total the book at the end of the period and post to the relevant accounts in the ledger. The VAT rate is 10 %; further analysis columns are not required.

19x6

Sept. 9   Inv. No. 3456 C. Gull £1,430 including VAT of £130. Account No. 66.

Sept. 10   G. A. Nett account no. 101, £715 including VAT.
P. Puffin account n. 120, £100. VAT must be added to this.

Sept. 11   F. Fulmar account no. 54, widgets £500, wotsits £230 and watsats £270. VAT must be added to these.

Sept. 12   C. Gull £220 including VAT.
S. Shag account no. 154, widgets £150 and wotsits £50. VAT to be added to these.

Sept. 13   G. T. Shearwater £242 including VAT, account no. 158.
P. Puffin £396 including VAT.

11.2 Enter the following purchases in the purchase day book of H. Hound. Columns are required for VAT, purchases, and expenses. The VAT rate is 25 %. The first invoice is numbered 20143, the rest follow consecutively. Total the book at the end of the period and post to the ledger.

19x8

Oct. 6   L. Lurcher stock items £550 including VAT, account no. 2054.
B. Asset bill for rent £600, account no. 2011.

Oct. 7   M. Blood stock items £1,075 including VAT, account no. 2025.

Oct. 8   P. Pointer stock items £450 including VAT, account no. 2093.

Oct. 9   E. Wolfe stock items £2,360 including VAT, account no. 2133.
B. Eagle stock items £1,235 including VAT, account no. 2030.

Oct. 10   M. Blood stock items £600, carriage £40, VAT £160.

11.3 Enter the following transactions in the appropriate day books. The VAT rate is 10 %, all the goods are subject to VAT and no further analysis columns are required. Total the day books at the end of the period and post them to the ledger. Prepare a trading account. Stock was valued as follows:
Jan. 1 £2,400, Jan. 31 £2,500

19x8

Jan. 1   Sales invoice no. 4296 to Z. Adams account no. 13 £2,340 excluding VAT.

Jan. 2   Purchases from: Y. Bede account no. 27 £4,510; X. Cart account no. 34 £561; W. Dee account no. 47 £979; all including VAT. Numerical sequence of invoices starts at 45632.

Jan. 5   Returned goods to W. Dee invoiced at £90 excluding VAT, raised debit note no. 86.

U. Exell account no. 59 purchased goods for £560 before VAT.

Jan. 7 Sales to: F. Vought account no. 227 £1,570; G. Timm account no. 206 £1,700; H. Susa account no. 199 £900; Z. Adams £1,250; all before VAT.

Jan. 11 Returns from Z. Adams, issue credit note no. Cr. 57 for a total of £111.

Jan. 17 Sales to H. Susa £4,000 and I. Rand account no. 182 £1,010 excluding VAT.

U. Exell returned goods as faulty, credit note for a total of £616 issued.

Purchased further goods from W. Dee £3,905 including VAT.

Jan. 18 Business closed down for fortnight.

11.4 Enter the following transactions in the appropriate day books. The VAT rate is 20% and all goods are subject to VAT. No further analysis columns are required. Total the day books at the end of the period and post them to the ledger. Prepare a trading account. Stock at start was valued at £6,700 and stock at close at £5,900.

19X0

April 1 Purchased goods from A. Sale account no. 197 £3,600 including VAT. Stamped purchase invoices in numerical order from 23456.

Sales to: M. Ludd account no. 76 £1,500; A. Lowry account no. 65 £2,500; and T. Land account no. 43 £2,000; VAT must be added to the invoices which start at number 7687.

April 2 Purchased goods from A. Sale £2,400 including VAT.

Goods returned by M. Ludd not according to specification, issued credit note no. 78 for a total of £600.

April 3 Returned goods to A. Sale, raised debit note no. 46 for total of £420.

Invoice received from V. Endor account no. 62 for £4,800 including VAT.

Sold goods for £2,700 before VAT to A. Lowry.

April 4 Purchased goods from A. Sale £1,200 including VAT.

Sales to: M. Light account no. 57 £1,600; and B. Long account no. 62 £3,300. VAT must be added to both invoices.

April 5 Returned goods to A. Sale, raised debit note for a total of £18.

Sold goods to P. Langly account no. 48 £1,400, VAT must be added to this.

11.5 From the following trial balance prepare a trading and profit and loss account and a balance sheet as at 31.3.19x1:

T. Tripp

Trial balance 31.3.19x1

	Dr. £	Cr. £
Capital 1.4.19x0		10,000
Sales		3,000
Purchases	900	
Land and buildings	7,200	
Fixtures and fittings	1,400	
Motor vehicles	1,200	
Stock 1.4.19x0	400	
Carriage in	100	
Carriage out	300	
Purchase returns		200
Sales returns	300	
Drawings	500	
Rates	200	
Wages	400	
Debtors	400	
Creditors		200
Cash	100	
	£13,400	£13,400

Stock-on-hand was valued at £500.

11.6 From the following trial balance prepare a trading and profit and loss account and draw up a balance sheet as at 30 April 19x8.

P. Uppet

Trial balance 30 April 19x8

	Dr. £	Cr. £
Capital (1 May 19x7)		8,951
Drawings	700	
Stock (1 May 19x7)	3,725	
Purchases	23,100	
Sales		39,426
Motor vehicles	1,475	
Cash on hand	110	
Creditors		4,925
Debtors	13,920	

	£	£
Bank overdraft		975
Wages and salaries	6,205	
Lighting and heating	310	
Equipment	3,600	
Carriage	231	
Sales returns	105	
Discount allowed (on sales)	286	
Discount received (on purchases)		315
Rent, rates and insurance	1,115	
Purchase returns		290
	£54,882	£54,882

Stock-on-hand was valued at £4,300

Chapter 12 THE JOURNAL

1 Explanation

For reasons of security it is advisable that all ledger entries are first recorded in a subsidiary book. The advantages of these books of prime entry have been enumerated in previous chapters. They help to regulate the book-keeping system, and together with a good system of internal control aid in the prevention and detection of errors and fraud. The day books and cash book contain the majority of entries for posting to the ledger, but there are certain transactions not covered by these books. These may be summarised as:

    (a)   Correction of errors.
    (b)   Credit sales and purchases of fixed assets.
    (c)   Sundry entries not covered elsewhere.
    (d)   Opening and closing entries.

All these transactions are first entered in a peculiar subsidiary book called the journal. This is not part of the double entry system, and transactions must be posted from it to both sides of the ledger.

As the journal covers all the complicated and unusual entries, there is the additional advantage that these can easily be checked by management and auditors. Any unusual transactions, and any transactions whereby amounts are written off, should be authorised by a responsible person other than the clerk who writes up the journal.

An example of a journal is shown below:

Date	Details	Dr. £	Cr. £
	Account to be debited	X	
	Account to be credited		X
	Explanation		

The debit entry must always be entered first. It is necessary to give some explanation about the entry, for instance if an error is being corrected there must be a reference to the original mistake. The details column is ruled off after each entry; the cash columns are not ruled off but used to check that the entries balance.

2   Correction of Errors

These can be subdivided into two main groups: errors discovered before a trial balance is extracted; and errors located after the trial balance has failed to balance and a suspense account has been opened. The suspense account is explained in Chapter 5.

2(a)   Errors discovered before a trial balance is extracted

All that is necessary is to reverse the incorrect entry and make the correct one. For example: a scrutiny of the fixed assets register revealed that a machine costing £5,000 had been left out of the machinery account. It was eventually located in the purchases account. The journal entry follows:

Date	Details	Dr. £	Cr. £
July 23	Machinery account	5,000	
	Purchases account		5,000
	Machine posted in error to the purchases account.		

The machine must be debited to the machinery account. The purchases account must be credited to reverse the original incorrect entry.

2(b)   Errors discovered after a suspense account has been opened

The correct entries must be made in the ledger and any balance posted to the suspense account. For example: after the opening of a suspense account to equalise the trial balance, the sales day book was found to be overcast by £1,000. This means that sales have been credited with an extra £1,000 which must be subtracted from the sales account.

Date	Details	Dr. £	Cr. £
July 31	Sales account	1,000	
	Suspense account		1,000
	Sales day book overcast by £1,000 during June.		

Sometimes there is a multiple mistake on one entry, but such errors are simple to correct as long as they are tackled methodically. For example: after the trial balance had been balanced by the opening of a suspense account, the sales returns for April, £250, were found to have been credited to the purchase returns account. To correct this the sales returns account must be debited with £250, and the status quo restored to the purchase account; the balance will be posted to the suspense account:

Date	Details	Dr. £	Cr. £
July 31	Sales returns account	250	
	Purchase returns account	250	
	Suspense account		500
	Correction of error whereby the sales returns for April were credited to the purchase returns account.		

A further example of a multiple error: after the trial balance had been balanced by the opening of a suspense account, the rent of £350 paid in March to the firm's solicitors was found to have been posted from the cash book to the legal expenses account as £530. To correct this the rent account must be debited with £350, the status quo restored to the legal expenses account and the balance posted to the suspense account:

Date	Details	Dr. £	Cr. £
July 31	Rent account	350	
	Suspense account	180	
	Legal expenses account		530
	Correction of error whereby rent for March of £350 was posted as £530 to the legal expenses account.		

3   Credit Sales and Purchases of Fixed Assets

These may be recorded in an additional analysis column in the sales and purchase day books. Great care must be taken to ensure that these entries are not posted to the sales and purchases accounts. If they are not recorded in the day books they must be entered in the journal.

3(a)   Purchase of Fixed Assets

The asset account will be debited and the account of the supplier credited. Sufficient details must be given to identify the particular asset referred to. For example: a farmer purchased a combine harvester for £25,000 and some additional fittings for the milking shed for £2,000 from Farm Supplies Ltd. The journal entry is:

Date	Details	Dr. £	Cr. £
May 19	Machinery account	25,000	
	Fixtures and fittings account	2,000	
	Farm Supplies Ltd		.27,000
	Being the purchase of combine harvester and sundry additions to milking shed invoice no. 56499.		

3(b) Sale of Fixed Assets

The sale of fixed assets are recorded, not in the sales account which contains only sales made in the course of trading, but in a special sale of fixed assets account. The profit or loss on the sales over year is transferred to the profit and loss account. For example: a car which cost £9,000 and had accumulated depreciation of £4,500 was sold to Ali's Autos Ltd. for £5,000. The journal entries are:

Date	Details	Dr. £	Cr. £
Feb. 28	Ali's Autos Ltd.	5,000	
	Sale of assets account		5,000
	Sale of assets account	9,000	
	Machinery account		9,000
	Prov. for Dep. machinery account	4,500	
	Sale of assets account		4,500
	Being sale of car registration no. XBL 123A		

4 Sundry Entries

The number of these should be kept to the minimum; the majority will probably relate to bad and doubtful debts.

4(a) Bad Debts

These occur for a number of reasons:
(a) The debtor disappears without trace.
(b) The debtor goes into liquidation (or in the case of an individual is adjudged bankrupt) with insufficient assets to cover his debts.
(c) The debtor may dispute the invoice and the amount involved may not warrant the expense of legal proceedings.
In any of these circumstances part or all of the outstanding debt will have to be

written off. This should only be done with management authorisation, or there could be scope for fraud.

For example: I. O. Yew was adjudged bankrupt, and had no assets. His account in the ledger had a balance of £350. The journal entry follows:

Date	Details	Dr. £	Cr. £
Dec. 3	Bad debts account	350	
	I. O. Yew account		350
	I. O. Yew adjudged bankrupt on Nov. 15; no further assets available for distribution.		

Debts should not be written off until there is no reasonable hope of recovery. While it seems probable but not certain that a debt will prove to be bad, a provision should be made against it. This is dealt with in more detail in Chapter 16. The bad debts account is an expense account which is charged to the profit and loss account.

5 Opening and Closing Entries

A journal entry is necessary when a ledger is first opened. It will list the assets and liabilities of the business and establish the amount of the proprietor's capital.
For example:
A. Trader wished to open proper books of account; he did not know his net worth but had made the following list of his assets and liabilities: Cash on hand £100. Bank account £5,000. Creditors: A Supplier £3,500. Debtors: T. Trite £250 and P. Prigg £1,200. Stock on hand £2,750. Fixtures and fittings £1,100, and a car valued at £3,500. The journal entry follows:

Date	Details	Dr. £	Cr. £
April 1	Fixtures and fittings	1,100	
	Motor vehicle	3,500	
	Stock	2,750	
	Debtors		
	T. Trite	250	
	P. Prigg	1,200	
	Cash at bank	5,000	
	Cash on hand	100	
	Creditor		
	A. Supplier		3,500
	Capital		10,400
	Being the assets and liabilities on hand on the opening of the books	£13,900	£13,900

5(a) Purchase of a Business

On many occasions when an established business is purchased, the purchaser will have to pay more than the total value of the individual assets for it. This is because he is buying not only stock and bricks but also (he hopes) a flourishing business with established customers and a reputation. The excess of the purchase price over the value of the assets is called goodwill. This is a fictitious or intangible asset. It is customary to show it on the balance sheet under fixed assets, and it must be amortised over a period of years. When a large concern takes over a smaller business and the purchase price includes an element of goodwill, the large firm may write off the goodwill immediately, especially if the amount is immaterial and there are sufficient reserves.

Example
Ernie Enterprise continued to expand. In order to diversify his interests he purchased a shop which sold car accessories. For £30,000 he received: premises valued at £20,000, fixtures and fittings £1,000, stock £5,000 and debtors of £2,500. His journal entry follows:

Date	Details	Dr. £	Cr. £
Nov. 5	Land and buildings	20,000	
	Fixtures and fittings	1,000	
	Stock	5,000	
	Debtors	2,500	
	Goodwill	1,500	
	Cash		30,000
	Being the purchase of the car accessory		
	shop from M. Carr.	£30,000	£30,000

Two points to note: goodwill is just the balancing figure, and the cash entry has to be shown in the journal to make the entry balance.

5(b) Closing Entries

Some firms like to record the transfer to the ledger accounts to the trading and profit and loss account in the journal. Although this follows the strict rule that all entries must appear in a subsidiary book it is a time-consuming job, and little benefit is gained as all the entries appear in the trial balance.

6 Computer-Based Systems

The hand-written journal is a vanishing species as even very small concerns can have a compact and inexpensive computer in the back office, to record transactions and produce accounts. However, journal entries have been dealt with in detail as they are the very entries required for computer input. The computer input dockets should be properly authorised, referenced and then filed, so that the entries can be checked if necessary.

7 Summary

(a) The journal is a book of prime entry recording those transactions not found in the day books or cash book.
(b) It is a subsidiary book and is not part of the double entry system.
(c) It is rapidly being outmoded by advancing technology but the method of writing entries is the same as for computer input.

Questions

12.1 Matt Moss was a tailor who also hired out clothes. Pursued by the Revenue and Vatman, he decided at last to consult an accountant and to open a ledger. On the back of a paper pattern he had scribbled the following details of his assets and liabilities: Cash on hand £250; bank £3,250; freehold shop £25,000; fixtures and fittings £1,250; bales of cloth £1,320; ready-to-wear clothes £1,680; car £5,500. After further questioning you ascertain that he owes £250 for electricity and £980 to Weavers Ltd., and that he has debtors of £2,280. Give the journal entry necessary to open his ledger and calculate his capital.

12.2 Sam Salt was a sailor who in retirement ran a small curio shop to eke out his pension. His business prospered and expanded; he realised that he needed financial advice. After many a sea shanty the following information was extracted from Sam: The shop is owned freehold; the value is estimated to be £20,000; fixtures and fittings £900; typewriter £100; safe £500; the rates, £1,150, have not been paid. M. Pepper, an old shipmate, lent him £5,000 to start the business; he keeps old papers in the safe and the petty cash tin containing £4,550 under the mattress—he does not trust banks. He recently bought a transit van for £6,950; there is a quantity of wood for making genuine antique furniture, £250; and his stock in the shop is valued at £1,330. He never allows credit. Give the journal entry necessary to open his ledger and calculate his capital.

12.3 Jeremiah Pond won £150,000, retired from the Air Force and purchased a small airline. For his winnings he obtained the lease on a shed, £5,000; two Dakota DC3 aircraft, £100,000; one pilot who was owed wages of £1,100; spare parts, £20,000; and one debtor, Abdul Ali, £5,500. Make the necessary journal entry to record Jeremiah's purchase of the business and calculate the amount paid for goodwill.

12.4 There is a debit balance of £945 on D. Bollam's account on November 1.

During the month he is adjudged bankrupt, and a cheque for £94.50 as a first and final payment is received from his trustee on November 29. Draft the journal entry to write off the bad debt and show Bollam's account for November.

12.5 You are required to deal with the following errors by means of journal entries:

(a) Wages amounting to £350 incurred in building extension to own house, charged to wages account.

(b) Goods sold on credit to A. Forbes for £500, debited in error to A. Ford's account.

(c) Total of sales returns day book £250 debited to the purchase returns account.

(d) Bank charges of £55 omitted from cash book.

(e) Typewriter £650 charged to office expenses.

(f) Car £2,500 sold for cash and proceeds credited to expenses. Cost of car £6,000. Accumulated depreciation £3,000.

12.6 On March 31 19x9 a trial balance was extracted from the ledger but the totals were

$$\begin{array}{cc} £ & £ \\ 54{,}339 & 55{,}279 \end{array}$$

All through April Fool's Day an army of clerks worked feverishly to discover the following errors:

(i) The total of purchases had been overcast by £10.

(ii) £66 received from P. Plumb had been debited to his account.

(iii) £245 paid to A. Rackham had been debited to R. Rachman.

(iv) A sales invoice for £81 had been posted to A. Bell's account as £18.

(v) £10 was debited to R. Rider when it should have been £1000.

(vi) Due to clerical error the balance on P. Piper's account was brought down as £615 instead of £715.

(a) Show the journal entries to correct these errors.

(b) Write up the suspense account and bring down the balance of undiscovered error.

12.7 Earl Grey extracted a trial balance on June 30 19x7. The debit side exceeded the credit side by £100. A suspense account was opened. The following mistakes were found later:

(i) A typewriter had been posted to the office machinery account as £670 instead of £760.

(ii) Cash discount of £10 allowed to T. Right had been omitted from his account.

(iii) Repairs to the central heating system, £600, had been charged to the freehold premises account.

(iv) £150 proceeds from the sale of an old typewriter had been debited to the office machinery account. The original cost of the asset was £300 and accumulated depreciation totalled £270.

(v) £1,120 bank interest charged had been entered in the cash book but not posted to the expense account.

(a) Show the journal entries to correct these errors.

(b) Write up the suspense account and bring down the balance of undiscovered error.

12.8 Name the accounts to be debited and credited in the following transactions and the book of prime entry.

Set out your answers under the following columns:

      Account debited   Account credited   Book of prime entry

(a) Sold goods to S. Scrimp on credit.

(b) Paid rent by cheque.

(c) Bought stock from Suppliers Ltd.

(d) Bought new car paid in cash.

(e) Purchased stationery for office use on credit from Universal Stationers.

(f) Wrote off D. Beggars account as a bad debt.

(g) Sold office desks for cash.

(h) Internal control fails to prevent theft. New employee removes petty cash float.

Chapter 13   THE BANK RECONCILIATION

1 Explanation

At intervals—monthly, weekly or as requested by customers—the bank will provide a statement of the firm's bank account. Unfortunately this is unlikely to agree with the balance in the cash book. There are three main reasons for this:

    (a) Items recorded in the cash book have not yet passed through the bank account.

    (b) There are items in the bank statement not yet recorded in the cash book.

    (c) There may have been an error in either cash book or bank statement.

So it is necessary to update the cash book to show the correct balance, and then to reconcile the two figures.

1(a) Items not yet Cleared Through the Bank Account

These consist of recent payments into the bank and cheques that have not been presented. There is no need to adjust the cash book and the items will appear on the bank reconciliation.

1(b) Items on the Bank Statement not Recorded in the Cash Book

There may be several of these as many transactions are dealt with directly by the bank.

(a) *Standing orders*

These are regular payments for specified amounts made directly by the bank. The firm should keep a list of such authorised payments and include them in the cash book.

(b) *Direct debits*

These are regular payments for varying amounts. They differ from standing orders

130

in that payment is initiated by the creditor. The firm must authorise the payment, and the creditor should inform the firm of the amount he has taken. This method is becoming more popular because it is cheap to administer and regular commitments such as subscriptions tend to increase annually.

(c) *Bank charges*
These are the charges made by the bank for administering the account. They are made at the manager's discretion but usually relate to the number of transactions on the account and the amount of the average balance.

(d) *Bank interest*
This is payable on loans and overdrafts. The amount charged is not usually a fixed percentage, as it often is in the case of personal loans such as Masterloan, but a fixed percentage over 'base'. Base rate is discussed below under the heading 'The Role of Banks'. Bank interest may be received on sums in deposit accounts. The banks usually make charges and pay interest at the half year, that is June and December 21.

(e) *Trader's credits*
These are credit transfers made by debtors. This is a popular method of payment in some industries. It obviates the need for cheques and so reduces the scope for fraud. The list of receipts must be carefully checked and posted to the debtors accounts.

(f) *Sundry direct transfers*
Some other receipts are commonly paid directly into the bank, for example dividends, interest on investments and insurance commission.

1(c) Errors

If the bank statement and cash book cannot be reconciled after the above factors have been taken into account the error must be located. It is most likely to be in the cash book and to be either arithmetical or a miscopying of a figure, for example '57' written as '75'. On very rare occasions an error is found in the bank statement. A cheque belonging to another party may be drawn on the firm's account. Even less frequently there is an arithmetical error; this would be due to computer malfunction, and the error likely to be gross.

2 Example

On June 30 Ernie Enterprise's cash book showed a debit balance of £550, while his bank statement of the same date showed a credit balance of £3,055. On scrutinising the two, the following discrepancies were revealed:
    (a) Cheques drawn but not yet presented to the bank totalled £2,155.
    (b) Bank charges of £25 had been made.
    (c) Credit transfers received and not entered in the cash book totalled £1,000.

(d)   A cheque for £125 drawn by Q. Street was returned marked 'refer to drawer'

(e)   A deposit of £300 made on June 29 had not been credited in the bank statement.

(f)   Interest of £200 had been charged on the bank loan.

The first point to note is that the bank statement shows Ernie's account from the point of view of the bank, and so is a mirror image of the account in the cash book. That means, if he has funds in the bank, the cash book will show a debit and the bank statement a credit balance. The next step is to adjust the cash book. Items (b), (c), (d) and (f) will affect this.

Dr.		Cash book			Cr.
June 30	Bal. b/d	550	Bank charges		25
	Credit transfers	1,000	Q. Street (ret. chq.)		125
			Interest		200
			Bal. c/d		1,200
		£1,550			£1,550
July 1	Bal. b/d	1,200			

Then the bank reconciliation can be made. It always starts with the balance on the bank statement and ends with the balance in the cash book.

Bank reconciliation

June 30

	£
Balance per bank statement	3,055
Add deposit not credited	300
Less cheques not presented	(2,155)
Balance per cash book	1,200

The reconciliation can be produced in the same format, even when there is an overdraft, if brackets are used to designate negative figures. On December 31 Bertie Wooster's cash book showed a credit balance of £1,700 while his bank statement showed a debit balance of £750. Both these figures indicate an overdraft. A comparison of the two revealed the following:

(a)   The insurance company had charged a direct debit of £150.

(b)   A deposit made on December 29 of £150 had not been credited by the bank.

(c)   Interest of £400 from investments had been credited directly to the bank account.

(d)   Cheques totalling £900 had not been presented to the bank.

(e)   A standing order to 'Leisure Magazine' for £50 had been omitted from the cash book.

First write up the cash book:

Dr.			*Cash book*			*Cr.*
Interest	400	Dec. 31	Bal. b/d		1,700
			Insurance D.D.		150
Bal. c/d	1,500		Leisure magazine		
			S.O.		50
	£1,900				£1,900
		Jan. 1	Bal. b/d		1,500

Then do the bank reconciliation:

Bank reconciliation

December 31

	£
Balance per bank statement	(750)
Add deposit not credited	150
Less cheques not presented	(900)
Balance per cash book	£(1,500)

3 The Role of Banks

Clearing banks

Most of the commercial banking business in England and Wales is dealt with by the clearing banks. These are the 'Big Four', Barclays, Lloyds, Midland, and National Westminster, together with Coutts & Co. (which is owned by National Westminster) and Williams and Glyn's. Other institutions also have access to clearing facilities; these include the Co-operative Bank and the Trustee Savings Bank. They are called clearing banks because they have established clearing houses where cheques paid into each bank but drawn on other clearing banks are sorted by computer.

Although these banks offer a great range of services, from taxation advice to the winding up of a late customer's estate, their main function is to enable money to keep circulating. Despite their incursion into the mortgage market they are essentially short term lenders.

Deposit accounts

Monies placed in deposit accounts attract interest at the current rate. There are restrictions on withdrawal from these accounts. As a general rule the longer the notice of withdrawal the higher the rate of interest. Large sums of money also attract higher rates of interest.

Overdraft

That is, when a current account is overdrawn. This must be negotiated with the bank manager. A limit is set on the amount of overdraft permitted. It is a most useful facility for covering small differences in the timing of payments and receipts. It is repayable on demand.

Loan

A fixed sum borrowed for a fixed period and for a specific purpose. The manager will usually require some security for the loan such as a mortgage on property or the deposit of investments. The interest charged is normally lower than on an overdraft.

Merchant banks

These are quite distinct from the clearing banks. The name arose because many of them originated in the nineteenth century as merchants and gradually changed to financing trade. Some of them do run current accounts for their customers but they concentrate on raising large deposits to lend in the medium term to industry. They supply finance to expanding firms and for export, and also arrange new issues of shares and debentures. They are also known as 'Acceptance Houses' as they accept bills of exchange on international transactions.

Base rate

The individual clearing banks quote the minimum rate at which they will lend, and this is known as their 'base' rate. The rate may vary from bank to bank.

Minimum Lending Rate (MLR)

The minimum rate at which the Bank of England will lend to the banks. It is set slightly above the normal market rate, and can be adjusted by the government to control the money supply. If it is raised, the banks are forced to charge higher interest rates: if it is lowered, the banks are able to charge lower interest rates. There are a great many other factors involved, but that is the broad pattern.

Debentures

A written acknowledgement issued by a company against a loan which is usually secured either on specific assets (such as land and buildings) or by a general charge on all the assets of the company. Interest is paid on debentures and usually a date is fixed for repayment.

Bill of Exchange

A written order by a drawer (usually the supplier) to a drawee (the purchaser) to pay a fixed sum on a given day to either the supplier or a third party. This becomes a negotiable instrument when it is accepted either by the drawee or merchant bank and can be discounted (sold) on the money market.

The advantage of this system is that it covers the often lengthy period between the dispatch and receipt of goods in international trade. The supplier is able to obtain money immediately by selling the bill of exchange, although it will be for less than its face value, and the purchaser does not have to pay until he has received the goods.

4 Summary

(a) The bank statement and cash book balances do not usually agree because of timing differences in the drawing and presenting of cheques and in the deposit and crediting of funds.

(b)   They will not agree if items have been omitted from the cash book or an error has been made.

(c)   First, the cash book must be adjusted.

(d)   Then a bank reconciliation can be prepared, starting from the balance on the bank statement and adjusting it to agree with the cash book.

Questions

13.1   Assuming that no mistakes have been made, give three reasons why the balance shown on your bank statement may disagree with the balance shown in your cash book.

13.2   On April 30 the balance on the bank statement of A. Company was £5,190 (credit) and the balance in the cash book £630 (debit). On comparison the following were found:

(a)   £2,500 deposited on April 29 had not been credited by the bank.

(b)   A credit transfer of £420 from B. Company had not been entered in the cash book.

(c)   A direct debit of £250 by A. Insurance Co. had not been entered in the cash book.

(d)   A standing order for £70 to a trade journal had been omitted from the cash book.

(e)   Cheques totalling £6,960 had not been presented to the bank.

Write up the cash book and prepare the bank reconciliation at April 30.

13.3   From the following information write up the cash book and prepare a bank reconciliation at June 30:

Balance per cash book £2,170 debit.

Balance per bank statement £2,990 credit.

Unpresented cheques £1,550.

Cheque returned marked 'refer to drawer' £120.

Dividends received by credit transfer not entered in cash book £210.

Deposit of £320 on June 28 not credited by bank.

Bank interest charged on loan account £500.

13.4   From the following information adjust the cash book and prepare a bank reconciliation at March 31:

Balance per cash book £650 credit (overdrawn).

Balance per bank statement £450 debit (overdrawn).

Unpresented cheques £970.

Standing order for subscription £150 omitted from cash book.
Credit transfer received by bank £160 not entered in cash book.
Deposit of £680 on March 28 not credited by bank.
Casting error in cash book, payments understated by £100.

13.5 From the following information adjust the cash book and prepare a bank reconciliation at December 31:

Balance per cash book £456 debit.
Balance per bank statement £240 credit.
Unpresented cheques £1,560.
Cheque returned marked 'refer to drawer' £920.
Direct debit by insurance company for £270 not entered in cash book.
Deposit of £190 on December 30 not credited by bank.
Transposition error in cash book: a cheque received for £105 was entered as £501.

13.6 From the following information adjust the cash book and prepare a bank reconciliation at June 30:

Balance per cash book £50 debit.
Balance per bank statement £120 debit (overdrawn).
Unpresented cheques £730.
Loan interest charged by bank £500.
Bank charges £35.
Deposit of £360 on June 29 not yet credited by bank.
Error in cash book, a cheque for £195 was received and discount allowed of £5; £200 was entered in the bank column.

13.7 The figures shown below appear on the bank statement for November of R. S. Tee:

		Dr. £	Cr. £	Balance £
Nov. 1				800
Nov. 4	861663	60		740
Nov. 7	861664	150		590
Nov. 7	861661	30		560
Nov. 8	Counter credit		430	990
Nov. 15	861662	50		940
Nov. 25	861665	120		820
Nov. 28	D. D. Insurance Co.	50		770
Nov. 29	Credit transfer P. Quail		200	970

His cash book shows the following:

Cheques 861661 and 2 were dated 27 October

Cash book

		£	£				£	Chq. No.
Nov. 1	Balance		720	Nov. 1	Rent		60	663
Nov. 8	Partridge	230		Nov. 4	B. Eagle		150	664
	Pheasant	200		Nov. 20	Basset Ltd.		20	665
			430	Nov. 21	Hound Bros.		40	666
Nov. 29	Grouse	80		Nov. 22	H. Whippet		20	667
	Snipe	140		Nov. 29	Balance		1,080	
			220					
			£1,370				£1,370	
June 1	Balance		1,080					

(a)   Check your cash book against the bank statement and bring the balance up to date.

(b)   Prepare a bank reconciliation statement on Nov. 30

(c)   How do you account for any difference which may remain?

Chapter 14 CONTROL ACCOUNTS

1 Explanation

In a large concern it is not unusual for the trial balance to disagree. Indeed, one may go further and say it is rare for it to agree. In these circumstances it is necessary to find ways of pinpointing the errors and reducing the area in which the search must be conducted. One way of doing this is to extract the trial balance at frequent intervals. Many large firms do produce monthly accounts; in this case any error will have arisen since the last trial balance. Nevertheless, in a multi-national concern a month's trading will comprise thousands if not millions of entries. Throughout the book, methods of preventing and detecting errors and fraud have been discussed. The bank reconciliation keeps a check on the bank account; the imprest system controls the petty cash; stock is counted on a regular basis; and a physical inspection is made of fixed assets and compared to the fixed asset register. This leaves debtors and creditors as the major uncontrolled figures, and it is here because of the great number of entries that many errors are located.

In Chapter 11 the advantages of reconciling creditors' statements to their accounts in the ledger were mentioned, but not all creditors produce statements. It is advisable to send regular statements to debtors and one may hope that if they are incorrect the debtor will complain, but this method cannot be relied on. If a debtor is informed that he owes less than is recorded in his own books he is unlikely to disagree. Another method is to check which invoices, payments received cover, and be warned by odd amounts or lump sums.

There is a further weapon in the armoury of the accountant, indefatigable in his war against errors, fraud and the wastage of man-hours in fruitless searches: the control account.

Control accounts can be designed within the double entry system. They are constructed from total figures and organised so that the ledger controlled is self-balancing. That is, the entries in the control account are on opposite sides to those in the ledger.

2   Debtors Control Accounts

Entries in the sales ledger to the individual debtors and control account are made as follows:

	Individual debtors	*Debtors control account*
(a)	Sales invoices from SDB (Dr.)	Total sales from SDB (Cr.)
(b)	Payments received from cash book (Cr.)	Total payments received from cash book (Dr.)
(c)	Discount allowed from cash book (Cr.)	Total discount allowed from cash book (Dr.)
(d)	Credit notes from SRDB (Cr.)	Total sales returns from SRDB (Dr.)
(e)	Bad debts, contras, refunds, from journal	Total if more than one debtor involved, otherwise individual entries from journal.

The control account in the sales ledger follows:

Dr.			*Debtors control account*			Cr.
		£				£
April 30	Cash received	60,750	April 1	Bal. b/d	57,500
	Discount allowed	600	April 30	Sales SDB	65,250
	April returns				
	SRDB	950			
	Bad debt J.	325			
	Bal. c/d	60,125			
		£122,750			£122,750
			May 1	Bal. b/d	60,125

The total of the individual debtors accounts should be £60,125. As the control account is designed within the double entry system, two accounts will be required. The other will be in the nominal ledger and will be a mirror image of the control account in the sales ledger.

Dr.			*Debtors control account (nominal ledger)*			Cr.
		£				£
April 1	Bal. b/d	57,500	April 30	Cash received	60,750
	April sales SDB	65,250		Discount allowed	600
				April returns	
				SRDB	950
				Bad debt J.	325
				Bal. c/d	60,125
		£122,750			£122,750
May 1	Bal. b/d	60,125			

This is the account which appears on the trial balance and it must agree with the control account in the sales ledger and the total of the debtors accounts. If the control account is not to be part of the double entry system there will be no control account in the sales ledger and the actual debtors accounts will be for memorandum purposes only.

3 Advantages of Control Accounts

(a) If the total of the individual debtors does not agree with the balance on the control account, then the ledger can be checked. If it does agree, the mistake is unlikely to be in the sales ledger and can be sought elsewhere.

(b) If the control accounts are prepared by a senior employee and the clerks who write up the ledger are denied access, then they can act as a check on the accuracy of the book-keeping and also deter fraud, as any entries made in the individual accounts must also be made in the control accounts.

(c) Control accounts will not reveal compensating errors within the same ledger or errors of commission (when an entry is posted to the wrong account), for example 'Rackman' instead of 'Rackham'.

4 Creditors Control Accounts

These can be set up along lines similar to the debtors control accounts. Total purchases, cash payments, discounts received and returns are posted to the control accounts. In the same way the control account in the purchases ledger will contain entries on the opposite side to the individual accounts, and the control account in the nominal ledger will contain the same entries on the same side as the individual accounts. The creditors control account in the nominal ledger will appear on the trial balance.

5 The Division of Sales and Purchase Ledgers

To control the accounts still further the ledgers can be divided into two or more sections, for example A–K and L–Z. A control account will be established for each section as described earlier. If the ledgers are split in this way it is possible to rotate the duties of the ledger clerks so that each one works for only a short period of time on each ledger section. This reduces the scope for fraud even further.

Strict control must be exercised over the amount any one debtor can owe (this is known as his credit limit), and over the length of time it takes to collect debts.

6 Creditors in the Sales Ledger

On occasion balances on individual accounts in the sales ledger may go into credit, for instance because goods have been returned or the same invoice has been paid twice. This will not affect the control account, but the amounts must be included with debtors on the balance sheet. For example: The balance on the debtors control account was £24,500 and on the creditors control account £30,125. The debtors account included £250 of credit balances. What figures will appear on the balance sheet?

The credit balances must be removed from debtors. This will increase the debtors figure by £250 to £24,750. The balance must be added to creditors which will also increase by £250 to £30,375.

There may also be debit balances on the purchases ledger in which case creditors and debtors will again both be increased.

7 Example

Ernie Enterprise decided to include debtors and creditors control accounts in his double entry system from January 1. From the following information write up the control accounts in the nominal ledger:

	£
Debtors Jan. 1	14,300
Creditors Jan. 1	12,500
Transactions in January	
Credit sales	16,100
Credit purchases	11,400
Receipts from debtors	15,650
Payments to creditors	11,150
Discount allowed	160
Discount received	110
Returns inwards	240
Returns outwards	720
Bad debts written off	610
Debit balances in sales ledger transferred to purchase ledger	125
Credit balances in purchase ledger transferred to sales ledger	90

Note: these contra accounts are explained in detail in Chapter 7.

Dr.		Debtors control account (nominal ledger)				Cr.
Jan. 1	Bal. b/d	14,300	Jan. 31	Cash received		15,650
Jan. 31	Jan. sales SDB	16,100		Discount allowed		160
				Jan. returns SRDB		240
				Bad debts J.		610
				Contras		
				Dr. bal. to Cr. control J.		125

					£
			Cr. bal. from Cr. control J.		90
			Bal. c/d		16,875
		£30,400			£30,400
Feb. 1	Bal. b/d	16,875			

Creditors control account (nominal ledger)

Jan. 31	Cash paid	11,150	Jan. 1	Bal. b/d	12,500
	Discount received	110	Jan. 31	Jan. Purchases	
	Jan. returns			PDB	11,400
	PRDB	720			
	Contras				
	Dr. bal. from Dr. control J.	125			
	Cr. bal. to Dr. control J.	90			
	Bal. c/d	12,195			
		£23,900			£23,900
			Feb. 1	Bal. b/d	12,195

Note the meaning of the reference initials: PDB, purchase day book; SDB, sales day book; PRDB, purchase returns day book (returns outwards); SRDB, sales returns day book (returns inwards); J, journal.

8 The Control Account Fails to Agree with the Sum of the Individual Balances

In this event the errors must be located and necessary adjustments made to both control and individual accounts.

Example
The debtors control account in the nominal ledger shows a balance of £9,675 while the sum of the individual debtor balances is £8,960. Working through the night a hapless clerk discovered the following errors:

(a) The total of the SRDB for June, £600, had been omitted from the control account.

(b) The sales day book for August was undercast by £100.

(c) A discount of £10 allowed to P. Price had not been posted to his account.

(d) A cheque for £95 had been received from H. Hunter but was posted to his account as £59.

(e) J. Zebedee with a balance of £86 on his account was omitted from the list of debtors.

(f) An invoice of £215 for I. Smyth had been posted to Y. Smith's account.

(g)   A bad debt of £250 had been written off in the journal but not posted to the debtors account at all.

(h)   A credit balance of £175 had been transferred from the creditors to the debtors ledger but not entered in the control account.

In the early hours of the morning she adjusted the control account and reconciled the schedule of debtors. She then tottered home to bed conscious of duty done.

Debtors control account (nominal ledger)

	£		£
Bal. b/d	9,675	a. SRDB June	600
b. SDB August	100	g. Bad debt J.	250
		h. Cr. bal. from Cr. control	175
		Bal. c/d	8,750
	£9,775		£9,775
Bal. b/d	8,750		

Adjustments to schedule of debtors

	£
Original total	8,960
c. Discount allowed P. Price	(10)
d. Transposition H. Hunter (95–59)	(36)
e. J. Zebedee	86
g. Bad debt	(250)
	£8,750

Notes

(i)   As the bad debt (g) had been omitted from both control and individual accounts it would not have affected the reconciliation.

(ii)   The posting of the invoice to the wrong account (f) will not affect either the total debtors or the control account.

9   Summary

(a)   Control accounts govern sections of the ledger, usually debtors and creditors accounts.

(b)   They are usually designed to work within the double entry system, so there are two control accounts for each section. One is in the nominal ledger and appears on the trial balance; the other remains with the section it controls so that the individual section is self-balancing.

(c)   The advantages of control accounts are:

(i)   An error made on a controlled section will be revealed when the control accounts do not agree, and only a relatively small part of the whole ledger need be checked.

(ii)   Together with a proper system of internal control they will help to prevent errors and fraud.

Questions

14.1 From the following details prepare the debtors control account in the nominal ledger:

	£
Feb. 1 Balance b/d	35,600
February transactions	
Credit sales	31,850
Receipts from debtors	36,115
Discount allowed	375
Returns inwards	435
Bad debt written off	25
Contras	
Debit balances transferred to creditors accounts	50
Credit balances transferred from creditors accounts	50

14.2 From the following details prepare the creditors control account in the nominal ledger:

March 1 Balance b/d	26,160
March transactions	
Credit purchases	25,780
Payments to creditors	24,540
Discount received	245
Returns outwards	430
Cash refund for payment made twice	55
Contras	
Debit balances transferred from debtors accounts	190
Credit balances transferred to debtors accounts	50

14.3 From the following information write up both the debtors and the creditors control accounts in the nominal ledger:

	£
April 1 Total debtors	18,900
Total creditors	12,210
Transactions in April	
Credit sales	19,750
Credit purchases	13,250
Receipts from debtors	19,600
Payments to creditors	11,800
Discount allowed	200
Discount received	120
Returns inwards	340

Returns outwards	1,075
Cheque returned marked 'refer to drawer'	110
Contras	
Debit balances in sales ledger transferred to purchase ledger	70
Credit balances in purchase ledger transferred to sales ledger	110

14.4 From the following information write up both the debtors and creditors control accounts in the nominal ledger:

	£
May 1 Total debtors	6,700
Total creditors	4,900
Transactions in May	
Credit sales	9,200
Credit purchases	6,300
Receipts from debtors (including £135 written off as a bad debt 3 years ago)	7,400
Payments to creditors	5,100
Cash payment made to S. Smith on the debtors ledger to close account	65
Discount allowed	745
Discount received	940
Returns inwards	470
Returns outwards	80
Dishonoured cheque	235
Bad debts written off	140
Debit balances transferred to purchase ledger	75
Credit balances transferred to sales ledger	125

14.5 The debtors control account in the nominal ledger had a balance of £56,955 while the sum of the debtors accounts was £56,950. On detailed examination of the accounts the senior clerk discovered the following errors:
(a) The receipts side of the cash book for August was undercast by £1,000.
(b) The discount allowed column for the same month was overcast by £100.
(c) A batch of sales invoices totalling £1,150 had been posted to the individual debtors accounts twice.
(d) The new junior had posted the credit balances transferred from the purchase ledger, £52, to the debit side of the control account.
(e) The account of G. Green with a balance of £300 had been included in the list of debtors twice.
(f) A bad debt of £905 had been written off but was posted to the control account as £509.
(g) A dishonoured cheque for £55 had been included in the control account but not posted to the individual debtors account.
Adjust the control account and prepare a reconciliation schedule of the individual debtors.

14.6   The creditors control account in the nominal ledger had a balance of £38,140 while the sum of the individual creditors was £38,250. Diligent searching located the following errors only hours before a visit from the Customs and Excise.

(a)   A creditor had been omitted from the list, £540.

(b)   The purchase day book for June had been undercast by £1,000.

(c)   The discount received during July, £340, had not been posted to the control account.

(d)   A purchase invoice, £360, had not been posted to T. Timm's account.

(e)   A contra of £150 from the sales ledger had been included in the control account but not posted to the individual ledger account.

(f)   The returns outwards for June had been posted to the control account as £201 instead of £102.

(g)   A cash refund of £101 received from a supplier on account of an overpayment had not been included in the control account.

Adjust the control account and reconcile the schedule of creditors.

Chapter 15 ACCRUALS AND PREPAYMENTS

1 Definition

An accrual may be defined as money owing for goods or services for which an invoice has not been received. A prepayment is money paid in advance for goods or services not yet received in full.

2 Explanation

In accountancy, the accruals concept ordains that the final accounts must show the income and expenditure relevant to the period, and not merely the receipts and payments. Certain goods and services may have been received but not invoiced and so not included in the ledger by the date to which the accounts are prepared. In order to follow the concept of accruals the cost of these must be included in the accounts. For example, if goods are included in stock, the cost of them must be included in purchases and creditors. There are some services which are normally paid for in arrears, for example, electricity, telephone calls and wages. The value of such services must be included in expenses and in creditors. Conversely, other goods and services may have been paid for in advance, for example, rates, rent and insurance. These must be extracted from expenses and included in debtors. The theory is that income must be matched with expenditure for the period covered by the accounts. This means that the period which has received the benefit of goods or services must be charged with the cost of them. It can be argued that this makes little difference in a time of relatively static prices, but in a time of high inflation the effect on the accounts can be considerable.

3 Example: Accrual Year 1

Rhoda Denn started business on January 1 19x1 and paid the following electricity bills:

	£	
April 28	250	quarter to March 31.
July 30	200	quarter to June 30.
Oct. 29	150	quarter to Sept. 30.

She prepares her accounts to December 31. In January 19x2 she received a.bill for £275 for the quarter to December 31. This latest bill must be taken into account, as the following entries in the ledger show:

Electricity account

19X1		£	19X1		£
April 28	Cash	250			
July 30	Cash	200			
Oct. 29	Cash	150			
Dec. 31	Accrual c/d	275	Dec. 31	Profit & loss a/c	875
		£875			£875
			19X2		
			Jan. 1	Accrual b/d	275

The double entry has been completed by putting both the entries in the same account. The credit balance brought down is money owing to the electicity board and will be included with creditors on the balance sheet. The full cost of the electricity for the year has been charged to the profit and loss account. If a bill is not received before the accounts are drawn up, an estimated figure may be used.

4   Example: Accrual Year 2

In 19x2 the following electricity bills were received and paid:

	£	
Jan.	275	quarter to Dec. 31 19X1.
April	300	quarter to March 31.
July	280	quarter to June 30.
Oct.	210	quarter to Sept. 30.

When the accounts were prepared early in January 19x3 no bill had been received for the last quarter's electricity but the figure was estimated to be £325. The entries in the ledger follow:

Electricity account

19X2		£	19X2		£
Jan. 31	Cash	275	Jan. 1	Accrual b/d	275
April 30	Cash	300			
July 31	Cash	280			

148

		£			£
Oct. 29	Cash	210			
Dec. 31	Accrual c/d	325	Dec. 31	Profit & loss a/c	1,115
		£1,390			£1,390
			19x3		
			Jan. 1	Accrual b/d	325

The bill paid at the end of January 19x2 cancels out the accrual at December 31 19x1. The amount charged to the profit and loss account for 19x2 is again the three paid bills relating to the year and the accrual at the year end. Any small adjustment necessary with an estimated figure happens automatically. If the bill to December 31 19x2 proves to be for £250 then £25 less will be charged to the profit and loss account for 19x3.

5   Example: Prepayment Year 1

When Rhoda moved into her new premises on January 1 19x1 she received a rates demand of £150 for the three months to March 31. No sooner had she paid it than she received another demand of £700 for the twelve months to March 31 19x2. The ledger entries follow:

Rates account

19x1			19x1		
		£			£
Jan. 31	Cash	150	Dec. 31	Prepayment c/d	175
April 30	Cash	700		Profit & loss a/c	675
		£850			£850
19x2					
Jan. 1	Prepayment b/d	175			

The rates of £700 relate to a whole year from April 1 19x1 to March 31 19x2, but Rhoda makes up her accounts to December 31. On that date she has paid the rates for the following three months, so the amount covering those three months:

$$£\ \frac{700}{4} = £175$$

should not be charged to the profit and loss account for 19x1, but be carried into 19x2. The double entry is completed by putting both the entries in the same account. The debit balance brought down represents a service owing to the business (in some circumstances the amount may even be repayable), and will be included with debtors on the balance sheet.

6   Example: Prepayment Year 2

In April 19x2 Rhoda received yet another rates demand of £800 for the year to March 31 19x3. The ledger entries follow:

Rates account

19x2		£	19x2		£
Jan. 1	Prepayment b/d	175	Dec. 31	Prepayment c/d	200
April 30	Cash	800		Profit & loss a/c	775
		£975			£975
19x3					
Jan. 1	Prepayment b/d	200			

The amount charged to the profit and loss account in 19x2 is composed of prepayment from the previous year £175 and three quarters of the bill paid in the current year £600, total £775.

7   Sundry Debtors

The business may be owed money for which an invoice will not be raised. An example of this would be money due in settlement of an insurance claim, or interest due on a deposit. In this event the sum due is treated in the same way as a prepayment.

Mary Gold makes up her accounts to March 31. She placed a large sum of money on deposit in September, and received interest of £2,500 on December 31 19x4. She calculated that the interest accrued to March 31 19x5 was £2,750. The ledger account follows:

Interest received account

19x5		£	19x4		£
			Dec. 31	Cash	2,500
			19x5		
March 31	Profit & loss a/c	5,250	March 31	Interest due	2,750
		£5,250			£5,250
April 1	Interest due	2,750			

The debit balance on the account was included in debtors on the balance sheet.

8   Sundry Stocks

Some firms keep substantial stocks of goods for consumption within the business and not for resale, for instance stationery, protective clothing, and uniforms. If the value of these stocks is material they must be included as assets on the balance sheet. Once stationery or protective clothing has been issued to the various departments it is rarely worth while to count and value it, but the stocks remaining in the store should be relatively easy to include in the accounts. The adjustment made to the ledger account is the same as for a prepayment.

For example: Mary Gold bought stationery for £1,300 in the year to March 31 19x5. The stock on hand was valued at £300. The ledger account follows:

Stationery account

19X5		£	19X5		£
March 31	Cash	1,300	March 31	Stock c/d	300
				Profit & loss a/c	1,000
		£1,300			£1,300
April 1	Stock b/d	300			

The stock of £300 was included on the balance sheet under sundry stock.

9 Example: Typical Question

When preparing accounts for a third party it is necessary to be able to adjust the trial balance to allow for any accruals and prepayments which have not yet been included in the ledger. The accounting staff of the business will write up the ledger later. When such adjustments are made it is essential to include both sides of the entry.

	Debit	Credit
Accrual	P & L	Creditors
Prepayment	Debtors	P & L

Rose Wyld extracted the following trial balance from her ledger on September 30 19X2.

Trial Balance

	£	£
Capital		80,000
Long term loan (7 years)		20,000
Land and buildings	60,000	
Motor vehicles	10,000	
Stock	15,000	
Debtors	25,000	
Creditors		50,000
Cash at bank	49,000	
Cash on hand	1,000	
Purchases	98,500	
Sales		120,000
Purchase returns		1,500
Sales returns	1,000	
Rent	1,000	
Rates	200	
Wages	11,800	
Insurance	300	
General expenses	200	
Interest on deposit		1,500
	£273,000	£273,000

Notes at September 30 19x2.
1. Stock was valued at £16,500.
2. £200 was owing for wages and £250 for rent.
3. Rates of £50 and insurance of £75 were prepaid.
4. Interest of £700 had accrued on the bank deposit account.
5. Depreciation of 25% is to be charged on the motor vehicles.
Prepare the final accounts as at September 30 19x2.

Workings
First adjust the trial balance. Only the relevant figures are shown below:

	Dr.		Cr.	
	Adj.	£	£	Adj.
Debtors	+ 50	25,000		
	+ 75			
Creditors			50,000	+ 200
				+ 250
Cash at bank	+ 700	49,000		
Rent	+ 250	1,000		
Rates	− 50	200		
Wages	+ 200	11,800		
Insurance	− 75	300		
Interest on deposit			1,500	+ 700
Provision for depreciation				+ 2,500
Depreciation	+ 2,500			
	+ 3,650			+ 3,650

It is essential that the adjustment columns balance. Total prepaid expenses to be included with debtors are £450, total accruals to be included in creditors are £125, and the interest due from the bank can be included in the bank balances.

THE FINAL ACCOUNTS

Rose Wyld

Trading and profit and loss account
30 September 19x2

	£		£
Stock 1.10.19x1	15,000	Sales	120,000
Purchases	98,500	Less returns	(1,000)
Less returns	(1,500)		
Stock 30. 9. 19x2	(16,500)		
Cost of sales	95,500		
Gross profit	23,500		
	£119,000		£119,000

	£			£
Rent	1,250	Gross profit		23,500
Rates	150	Interest		2,200
Wages	12,000			
Insurance	225			
Depreciation	2,500			
General expenses	200			
Net profit	9,375			
	£25,700			£25,700

Balance Sheet
as at 30 September 19x2

Fixed assets	£	£	£
	Cost	Dep.	NBV
Land and buildings	60,000	—	60,000
Motor vehicles	10,000	2,500	7,500
	70,000	2,500	67,500
Current assets			
Stock	16,500		
Debtors	25,125		
Cash at bank	49,700		
Cash on hand	1,000		
	92,325		
Less current liabilities			
Creditors	50,450		
Net working capital			41,875
Net value of assets			£109,375
Capital			89,375
Long-term loan			
(repayable in 7 years)			20,000
Capital employed			£109,375

10 Summary

(a) An accrual is an amount due for which an invoice has not been received.

(b) A prepayment is an amount paid in one financial period which relates to goods or services receivable in a subsequent financial period.

(c) Amounts accrued increase the expenditure for the period and are included on the balance sheet as a liability.

(d) Amounts prepaid decrease the expenditure for the period and are included on the balance sheet as an asset.

(e) The accrual concept is fundamental to the preparation of the accounts. It ensures that all benefits actually received and only benefits actually received are included in the accounts.

Questions

15.1 W. Briar paid £30,300 in wages during the year ended 30 June 19x3. £1,250 is due but unpaid in respect of wages at that date. The accrual in 19x2 was £900. Show the wages account in the ledger for the year ended 30 June 19x3 including the transfer to profit and loss and any balance carried down.

15.2 D. Thorn paid insurance bills totalling £1,600 during the year ended 31 March 19x7. All his insurances run annually from July 1. The prepayment in 19x6 was £300. Show the insurance account in the ledger for the year ended 31 March 19x7 including the transfer to profit and loss and any balance carried down.

15.3 The lighting and heating account from the ledger of Harry Hedge is shown below:

Lighting and heating account

19x5			19x5	
Jan. 1	Stock of oil b/d	250	Jan. 1 Electricity accrual b/d	125
Feb. 28	Oil	1,100		
March 31	Electricity to Feb. 28	350		
June 30	Electricity to May 31	250		
Aug. 31	Oil	1,250		
Sept. 30	Electricity to Aug. 31	115		
Dec. 31	Electricity to Nov. 30	285		

Notes

It was estimated that £150 worth of electricity was consumed in December 19x5. The oil on hand on December 31 19x5 was valued at £325. Close off the account at December 31 19x5, transfer the appropriate amount to profit and loss and bring down the balances.

15.4 From the following information write up the telephone account in the ledger for the year ended March 31 19x9. Show the transfer to profit and loss and bring down the balance.

An accrual of £115 was brought down on 1 April 19x8 comprising £100 rental paid in advance, and an estimated £215 due on calls. Bills are paid one month in arrears; the dates to which they refer follow: June 30 £800; September 30 £775; December 31 £815; March 31 £850. The rental increased to £180 a quarter from March 1 19x9.

15.5 Basil Brush, an airline pilot, started a decorating business on April 1 19x2 with £2,500 capital. He pursued his business in his spare time. He took his rudimentary records to an accountant who produced the following trial balance at March 31 19x3:

	£	£
Purchases of paint, brushes, etc.	800	
Estate car	1,500	
Scaffolding	400	
Car expenses	500	
Insurance	250	
Rent of garage	300	
Wages to wife for clerical work	1,000	
Telephone	150	
Sundry expenses	75	
Personal expenses paid from bank	2,000	
Cash at bank	575	
Receipts from clients		5,050
Capital		2,500
	£7,550	£7,550

Basil reckons that the scaffolding will last ten years and the car five. There is £75 rent outstanding, and an estimated £20 due for telephone calls. Insurance of £100 is prepaid, a customer owes him £650, and he has a stock of paint valued at £175.

Prepare a profit and loss account and a balance sheet for Basil's first year of trading.

15.6 The following trial balance was extracted from the books of Eleanor Field at 31 May 19X1, her financial year-end:

Trial Balance

	£	£
Furniture, fittings and equipment	8,000	
Accumulated depreciation on furniture, fittings and equipment to 31st May 19X0		1,925
Sales		48,085
Purchases	33,340	
Stock 1 June 19X0	8,350	
Rent, rates and insurance	1,240	
Selling expenses	4,850	
Returns outwards		440
Returns inwards	600	
Bad debts	350	
Discounts allowed and received	1,250	
Debtors	4,450	
Administrative expenses	2,035	
Creditors		3,900
Cash in hand	35	
Cash at bank	2,350	
Capital		12,500
	£66,850	£66,850

Prepare the final accounts for the year ended 31st May 19x1 with a Balance Sheet at that date.

Notes at 31 May 19x1
(a) Stock was valued at £9,930.
(b) £350 commission to salesmen was due but unpaid.
(c) Rates of £135 were prepaid.
(d) Depreciation of 10% on cost is to be charged on all fixed assets.

15.7 Prepare a trading and profit and loss account and a balance sheet from Percival's trial balance as at April 30 19x4:

	£	£
Capital		30,000
Cash on hand	250	
Cash at bank	11,050	
Freehold premises	20,000	
Motor vehicles	6,000	
Fixtures and fittings	900	
Wages and salaries	7,500	
Light and heat	750	
Interest received		700
Sundry expenses	150	
Stationery	110	
Discount allowed and received	190	230
Purchases	17,000	
Sales		25,500
Returns in and out	500	150
Drawings	1,500	
Stock	1,200	
Carriage in	125	
Carriage out	195	
Debtors and creditors	2,500	3,340
Long term loan		10,000
	£69,920	£69,920

Notes at April 30 19x4
(a) Stock was valued at £3,400.
(b) £500 was owing for wages, and £150 for electricity.
(c) Interest of £175 was due from the bank deposit account.
(d) There was a stock of stationery valued at £50.
(e) Depreciation is to be written off on a straight-line basis at the following rates: freehold premises over 50 years, fixtures and fittings over 10 years, and motor vehicles over 5 years.

Chapter 16   RESERVES AND PROVISIONS BAD DEBTS AND PROVISION FOR DOUBTFUL DEBTS

1   Definition

A reserve is an allocation or appropriation of profits. A provision is any amount written off or retained to provide for depreciation, renewals or loss in the value of assets, or is a charge against profits for expenditure incurred but not yet paid.

The main distinction between a reserve and a provision is that a provision reduces the net profit, while a reserve is represented by surplus assets.

2   Reserves

Reserves represent profit which has not been withdrawn by the proprietor, the partners, or in a limited company the shareholders.

2(a)   Capital Reserves

In a limited company certain reserves may not be available for distribution to shareholders as dividends because they represent a capital profit. These are known as capital reserves. An example of a capital profit is the increase in value of premises; although these may be worth considerably more than the company paid for them, the company does not receive any immediate benefit from this. It would not be sensible to distribute this profit as dividends, indeed it is most unlikely that there would be any cash available to do so.

2(b)   Revenue Reserves

Other reserves represent undistributed profit and these may be paid as dividends if the directors think fit. It would not be wise to distribute the entire profits as they will be needed to fund expansion and to purchase fixed assets.

3 Bad Debts

Any large firm and many smaller ones suffer from bad debts from time to time. Some reasons for this are listed in Chapter 12. The debt may be legally enforceable but this is of no use if the debtor cannot be found or has no assets. In this event there is no alternative but to write off the debt. A bad debts account is opened and debited with the amount written off, and the debtors account is credited. At the year end the bad debts are charged to the profit and loss account.

Example
Bertie Wooster at last accepts that, as the inquiry agents have been unable to trace Mr. Abdullah, he will have to write off the £4,600 on his account as a bad debt.

Debtors Ledger

19X2		£	19X3		£
March 1	Balance b/d	4,600	Jan. 31	Bad debt	4,600

Bad Debts Account

19X3		£	19X3		£
Jan. 31	Abdullah	4,600	Sept. 30	Profit & loss a/c	4,600

Profit and Loss Account (extract)
September 30 19X3

Bad debts	4,600

4 Provision for Doubtful Debts

A debt should not be written off until there is no reasonable hope of recovery, but it would not be prudent to give the full total of debtors in the accounts when one knows from experience that not all the money will be recovered. To overcome this problem a provision is made for the doubtful debts. This may comprise both particular debts which are suspect and a general provision of a certain percentage of the outstanding debts. The percentage will be determined by past experience.

The provision for doubtful debts account works in the same way as the provision for depreciation account. It is a negative asset account with a credit balance which is subtracted from the total of debtors on the balance sheet.

Example
Miss Crawley opened a children's clothes shop 'Creepy Crawly' on January 1 19X1. She decided to create a provision for doubtful debts of 5% of debtors. Her debtors at the year end follow:

31 December 19x1   £5,000
31 December 19x2   £6,000
31 December 19x3   £5,500

Provision for doubtful debts account

Dr.			19x1		Cr.
		£			£
			Dec. 31	Profit & loss a/c (5% of £5,000)	250
19x3			19x2		
Dec. 31	Profit & loss a/c (adj. to bring bal. to 5% of £5,500)	25	Dec. 31	Profit & loss a/c (adj. to bring bal. to 5% of £6,000)	50
	Balance c/d	275			
		£300			£300
			19x4		
			Jan. 1	Balance b/d	275

Profit and loss account (extract)
December 31

	19x1	
Provision doubtful debts	250	
	19x2	
Provision doubtful debts	50	
	19x3	
	Provision doubtful debts	25

Balance Sheet as at December 31 (extract)
19x1

Current assets	£	£
Debtors	5,000	
Less provision for doubtful debts	(250)	
		4,750

19x2

Current assets	£	£
Debtors	6,000	
Less provision for doubtful debts	(300)	
		5,700

19x3

Current assets	£	£
Debtors	5,500	
Less provision for doubtful debts	(275)	
		5,225

It will be noted that although the balance on the provision for doubtful debts account appears on the balance sheet, only the adjustment appears in the profit and loss account, and this adjustment may be either a debit or a credit.

When it is necessary both to write off bad debts and to create or adjust the provision for doubtful debts, the bad debts must be written off first and the provision calculated on the reduced debtor balance.

5   Credit Control

Bad debts may be reduced to a minimum by effective credit control. Many large firms have a department devoted to this. The first step is to vet the prospective debtor for credit-worthiness.

He may be asked to give references from other traders and his bank. However, such references tend to be vague because of the laws against libel. In the case of a limited company the accounts may be scrutinised at Companies House. The most efficient method is to use an enquiry agency such as Dun and Bradstreet, who will ascertain whether legal proceedings have ever been taken against him for the recovery of a debt. They will also make general enquiries about his financial standing.

Once the decision to sell goods on credit has been made, an individual credit limit should be set for each customer. If strictly adhered to it will limit the amount of any single bad debt, and should be instrumental in realising the debts when debtors wish to order further goods. A careful watch should be kept on overdue debts, and these must be followed up. To facilitate this an analysis may be made of the ageing of debtors, whereby total figures are produced for debtors in monthly age-bands, up to one month old, from one to two months old, from two to three months old, etc. If credit control is improving, the percentage of total debtors in the one-month-old band will increase and the percentage of debtors over six months old will decrease. If credit control is ineffective, the reverse will happen. Once debts begin to age they become more difficult to collect. Nevertheless, if credit control is very strict a number of good customers will be lost; if it is lax the amount of bad debts may be considerable. The skill in credit control lies in finding the middle road between the two extremes. Statistical methods of doing this are considered in Chapter 19.

6   Provision for Discounts Allowed

Many firms offer cash discounts to customers who pay within a specified time, and this is discussed in detail in Chapter 10. At the year-end some debtors will be eligible for this discount and provision may be made for it.

It is most sensible to regard this provision as an accrual in the discount allowed account.

The discount is calculated only on those debtors who are eligible for it, that is if a 2% cash discount is allowed terms 30 days, the discount should be calculated on outstanding sales invoices for the last 30 days. The complication of some of these debts being doubtful is unlikely to occur as they are recent by definition. If it should happen, for instance because a receiver has just been appointed, then no provision will be required for discount allowed.

The provision is subtracted from the total of debtors on the balance sheet.

Example

Miss Crawley allows a cash discount of 2% terms 30 days; the ageing analysis of her debtors over the last three years follows:

	1 mth £	2 mths £	3 mths £	3–6 mths £	over 6 mths £	Total £
31 Dec. 19x1	2,500	2,000	250	150	100	5,000
31 Dec. 19x2	3,000	2,250	450	225	75	6,000
31 Dec. 19x3	2,750	2,000	475	200	75	5,500

The discounts allowed were: 19x1 £360, 19x2 £400, 19x3 £420

Dr.		Discount allowed account				Cr.
19x1			£	19x1		£
Dec. 31	Cash book		360			
	Prov. for discount c/d (2% £2,500)		50	Dec. 31	Profit & loss a/c	410
			£410			£410
19x2				19x2		
Dec. 31	Cash book		400	Jan. 1	Prov. for discount b/d	50
	Prov. for discount c/d (2% £3,000)		60	Dec. 31	Profit & loss a/c	410
			£460			£460
19x3				19x3		
Dec. 31	Cash book		420	Jan. 1	Prov. for discount b/d	60
	Prov. for discount c/d (2% £2,750)		55	Dec. 31	Profit & loss a/c	415
			£475			£475
				19x4		
				Jan. 1	Prov. for discount b/d	55

Balance Sheet as at December 31 (extract)

19x1

	£	£
Current assets		
Debtors	5,000	
Less provision for doubtful debts	(250)	
Less provision for discounts	(50)	
		4,700

19x2

	£	£
Current assets		
Debtors	6,000	
Less provision for doubtful debts	(300)	
Less provision for discounts	(60)	
		5,640

19x3

	£	£
Current assets		
Debtors	5,500	
Less provision for doubtful debts	(275)	
Less provision for discount	(55)	
		5,170

On a theoretical level it may be argued that the general provision for doubtful debts should be subtracted from the debts eligible for discount, before the provision for discount is calculated. However, although a general provision is made against all outstanding debts, it is the older debts which will prove uncollectable. The general provision is as much against disputes over invoices, claims of overcharging and faulty workmanship, as against the mysterious disappearance and inability to pay of debtors. It is possible that all the cash discounts will be claimed, and prudence dictates that provision must be made for these.

It would not be prudent to make an allowance for the cash discounts which the business may receive from creditors. The business may be in the habit of discharging its debts so as to obtain maximum benefit from such discounts, but this must be considered as an unrealised profit. Only realised profits may be included in the profit and loss account.

7 Example: Typical Question

On occasion adjustments for bad debts, doubtful debts and cash discounts are made after the trial balance has been drawn up. In this event it is essential that both sides of the adjustment are included in the trial balance. The accounting staff will write up the ledger at a later date. The entries are:

	Debit	*Credit*
Bad debts written off	P & L	Debtors
Increase provision for doubtful debts	P & L	Provision for doubtful debts on balance sheet

| Decrease provision for doubtful debts | Provision for doubtful debts on balance sheet. | P & L |
| Provision for cash discount | Discount allowed in P & L | Provision for discount on balance sheet |

Thomas Thorn extracted the following trial balance from his ledger on June 30 19x3:

Trial Balance

	£	£
Capital July 1 19x2		20,000
Freehold land and buildings	15,000	
Fixtures and fittings	1,500	
Motor vehicle	6,000	
Provision for depreciation freehold property		600
Provision for depreciation fixtures and fittings		300
Provision for depreciation motor vehicle		3,000
Bad debts written off during year	600	
Provision for doubtful debts July 1 19x2		500
Drawings	3,500	
Purchases and sales	60,000	90,000
Discount allowed and received	1,200	900
Debtors and creditors	9,000	5,000
Stock July 1 19x2	6,000	
General Expenses	300	
Wages	7,000	
Rates	800	
Depreciation	450	
Cash at bank and in hand	8,950	
	£120,300	£120,300

Notes at June 30 19x3

(a) Stock was valued at £7,000

(b) Depreciation has been provided for on the land and buildings and on the fixtures and fittings, but not on the motor vehicle which is being amortised over four years.

(c) Rates of £600 were prepaid.

(d) A debt of £50 which is over a year old is to be written off as bad.

(e) A receiver and manager was appointed to Joe Bloggs Ltd. on July 3 19x3 and his debt of £950 must be considered doubtful. £600 of this balance arose from sales in June 19x3.

(f) The general provision for doubtful debts is to be adjusted to 2% of debtors.

(g) Thomas allows a cash discount of 2½% terms 30 days; the outstanding debts

which arose from sales in June 19x3 are £5,000.
Prepare the final accounts as at 30 June 19x3.

Workings
First, adjust the trial balance. Only the relevant figures are shown below.

		Dr.		Cr.	
Note		Adj.	£	Adj.	£
2	Depreciation	+ 1,500	450		
	Prov. for depreciation vehicles			+ 1,500	3,000
3	Rates	− 600	800		
4	Bad debts	+ 50	600		
3	Debtors	+ 600			
4		− 50	9,000		
5	Provision for doubtful debts			+ 950	500
6				− 340	
5	P & L	+ 950			
6		− 340			
7	Provision for cash discount			+ 110	
	Discount Allowed	+ 110	1,200		
		£2,220		£2,220	

It is essential that the adjustment columns balance. The provision of £1,110 for doubtful debts comprises £950 for a specific debt and £160 for a general provision of 2 % on debtors of £8,000. That is, debtors of £9,000 less the bad debt written off (£50) and the doubtful debt specifically provided for (£950).

The provision for cash discount is based on debts arising from sales in June (£5,000) less the debt which has been specifically provided against (£600): these total £4,400. 2¼% of £4,400 equals £110.

Dr.			*Capital account*			Cr.
19x3				19x2		
		£				£
June 30	Drawings	3,500	July 1	Balance b/d		20,000
			19x3			
	Balance c/d	36,380	June 30	Net profit		19,880
		£39,880				£39,880
			July 1	Balance b/d		36,380

The Final Accounts

Thomas Thorn

Trading and profit and loss account

30 June 19x3

Stock 1 July 19x2	6,000	Sales	90,000
Purchases	60,000		
Stock 30 June 19x3	(7,000)		
Cost of sales	59,000		
Gross profit	31,000		
	£90,000		£90,000
Bad debts	650	Gross profit	31,000
Discount allowed	1,310	Discount received	900
Provision for doubtful debts	610		
General expenses	300		
Wages	7,000		
Rates	200		
Depreciation	1,950		
Net profit	19,880		
	£31,900		£31,900

Balance Sheet

as at 30 June 19x3

	£ Cost	£ Dep.	£ NBV
Fixed assets			
Land and buildings	15,000	600	14,400
Fixtures and fittings	1,500	300	1,200
Motor vehicles	6,000	4,500	1,500
	22,500	5,400	17,100
Current assets			
Stock		7,000	
Debtors	9,550		
Less provision for doubtful debts	(1,110)		
Less provision for cash discount	(110)		
		8,330	
Cash at bank and in hand		8,950	
		24,280	
Less current liabilities			
Creditors		5,000	
Net working capital			19,280
Net value of assets			£36,380
Capital employed			£36,380

8 Summary

(a)   A provision reduces net profit while a reserve is an appropriation of surplus assets.

(b)   Both provisions and reserves must be shown on the balance sheet.

(c)   The provision for doubtful debts is made up of two parts, specific provision for particular debts which appear doubtful and a general provision against the remaining debtors based on a percentage determined by experience.

(d)   Where the business allows a cash discount a provision should be made against debts which are eligible for the discount. Any debts which are considered to be doubtful must be subtracted from the debts eligible for discount before the calculation is performed.

Questions

16.1   At the year end the control account shows that debtors total £15,780 and the provision for doubtful debts account stands at £350. Two debts are considered to be irrecoverable, S. Swindle £200 and T. Twister £380. The provision for doubtful debts is to be adjusted to 2½% of debtors. Show the provision for doubtful debts account in the ledger and the debtors on the balance sheet.

16.2   Harry Smiles allows a cash discount of 2½% terms 30 days. His debtors for the past three years were as follows:

	1 mth. £	2 mths. £	over 2 mths. £	Total £
31 Dec. 19x4	1,600	900	800	3,300
31 Dec. 19x5	2,000	1,000	900	3,900
31 Dec. 19x6	2,400	950	850	4,200

Discounts allowed were 19x4 £410, 19x5 £430, 19x6 £460. Write up the discount allowed account in the ledger for the three years and show the entry for debtors in the balance sheets.

Comment on the success of Harry's credit control.

16.3   William Woeful allows a cash discount of 3% terms 30 days. His debtors for the past three years were as follows:

	1 mth. £	2 mths. £	over 2 mohs. £	Total £
30 June 19x4	2,500	1,250	1,300	5,050
30 June 19x5	2,600	1,200	1,500	5,300
30 June 19x6	2,650	1,300	1,750	5,700

Discounts allowed were 19x4 £625, 19x5 £630, 19x6 £615. On 30 June 19x5 there was a specific provision for doubtful debts of £425, of which £200 related to debts arising in June 19x5. These debts were written off in March 19x6. Show the discount allowed account in the ledger for the three years and the entry for debtors in the balance sheet.

Comment on the success of William's credit control.

16.4 On 31 March 19x5 Millicent Mousley decided to create a provision for doubtful debts based on 5% of debtors and a provision for cash discounts based on 2% of eligible debtors, and to maintain the provisions at those percentages at the end of each financial year. Relevant details for three financial years follow:

Debtors	1 mth.	2 mths.	over 2 mths.	Total
	£	£	£	£
31 March 19x5	6,500	3,000	3,500	13,000
31 March 19x6	6,900	3,400	4,400	14,700
31 March 19x7	7,350	4,050	3,100	14,500

Bad debts included above to be written off, 19x5 £350 all over two months old; 19x6 £300 of which £100 is less than four weeks old; 19x7 £500 of which £50 is less than 1 month old.

Discount allowed 19x5 £780, 19x6 £880, 19x7 £860.

Write up the ledger accounts for discount allowed and provision for doubtful debts and show the entry for debtors in the balance sheet for each of the three years.

16.5 Matilda Walsing, a manufacturer of kangaroo tail soup, decided to raise a general provision for doubtful debts of $2\frac{1}{2}$% of debtors from April 30 19x9. At that date specific provision was made against the following debts: Sid Neah £75, E. Wooloomool £50, Alice Springs £85, and G. Long £100. The remaining debtors totalled £12,000. During the year ended April 30 19x0 no further sales were made to the above debtors. Sid Neah was declared bankrupt and there were no assets. Alice Springs paid her account in full, G. Long made an arrangement with his creditors to pay 75 pence in the pound, while E. Wooloomool promised to pay as soon as his boomerang came back so a specific provision was kept against his debt. Total debtors at April 30 19x0 were £13,050. Write up the provision for doubtful debts account and the bad debts account in the ledger and show the entry for debtors in the balance sheet as at April 30 19x9 and 19x0.

16.6 After drawing up the trading and profit and loss accounts the following balances remained in the ledger of Mildred Musselwhite at August 30 19x7:

	£	£
Capital		20,000
Net Profit for year to 30.8.x7		1,900
Leasehold property	10,000	
Plant and machinery	5,000	
Motor vehicles	7,000	

Provision for depreciation at 1.9.x6		
Leasehold property		3,000
Plant and machinery		2,500
Motor vehicles		1,750
Stock	6,500	
Debtors	7,200	
Provision for doubtful debts		300
Cash at bank and in hand	1,200	
Creditors		7,450
	£36,900	£36,900

Mildred took her accounts to Douglas, an accountant, and he insisted that the following adjustments be made.

(a) The lease for the property is for ten years from 1 September 19x3 and depreciation must be provided for the current year.

(b) Depreciation must be provided on a straight-line basis for the plant and machinery, expected life 10 years, and the motor vehicles, expected life 4 years.

(c) One of the debts for £200 is over five years old and must be written off as bad.

(d) The provision for doubtful debts is to be adjusted to 5% of debtors. Draw up Mildred's balance sheet as at August 30 19x7.

16.7 The following trial balance was extracted from the ledger of Vincent Vinn on December 31 19x2. Prepare the trading and profit and loss account and the balance sheet as at December 31 19x2 (after taking the notes into consideration):

	£	£
Capital		19,000
Freehold land and buildings	12,000	
Fixtures and fittings	1,500	
Motor car	9,000	
Provision for depreciation on motor car		3,375
Purchases and sales	47,000	70,625
Rent received		1,200
Drawings	4,250	
Vehicle expenses	900	
Debtors and creditors	8,350	8,000
Returns in and out	700	450
Discount allowed and received	700	500
Bad debts	600	
Provision for doubtful debts 1.1.x2		140
Stock	5,500	
Wages and salaries	8,600	
Rates	1,500	
General expenses	1,790	
Cash in hand and at bank	900	
	£103,290	£103,290

Notes

(a). Stock-on-hand 31 December 19x2 £7,000.
(b)   Rates paid in advance £375.
(c)   Wages and salaries accrued £450.
(d)   A debt of £150 is considered to be irrecoverable.
(e)   The provision for doubtful debts is to be adjusted to 2% of debtors.
(f)   A room in the building was let to a tenant who owed £150 rent.
(g)   Depreciation is to be provided on the car at 25% on cost.

16.8   Gerald the Mole works a gold mine in Wales, in business by himself. This trial balance was extracted from his somewhat grubby ledger on March 30 19x4:

	£	£
Capital		30,000
Drawings	6,900	
Plant and machinery	4,300	
Buildings	4,000	
Quarry	2,500	
Stock of gold for sale 1 April 19x3	2,000	
Insurance	1,200	
Sundry mining expenses	650	
Sales		30,000
Power for mine	1,700	
Miner's wages	7,500	
Motor car	8,500	
Vehicle expenses	1,200	
Debtors	6,300	
Cash in hand and at bank	5,500	
Office expenses	2,750	
Office salary	5,000	
	£60,000	£60,000

From this his accountant, Carla Count, extracted the following information:
(a)   The stock of gold on hand was valued at £6,000.
(b)   The plant and machinery was purchased in April 19x3 and has an estimated life of ten years after which it will be scrapped.
(c)   The motor car is to be written off over four years.
(d)   A debt of £300 is considered irrecoverable.
(e)   A provision is to be made for doubtful debts amounting to 2% of debtors.
(f)   Insurance paid in advance is £300.
(g)   Unpaid mining expenses total £100.
(h)   Unpaid office expenses total £250.
(i)   The rise in the price of gold during the year, and the discovery of additional high-quality veins of ore, necessitate a revaluation of the quarry to £25,000.

Prepare Gerald's trading and profit and loss account and his balance sheet as at 30 March 19x4.

Chapter 17 STATEMENTS OF THE SOURCE AND APPLICATION OF FUNDS CASH FLOW STATEMENTS

1 Definition

A statement of the source and application of funds shows from where funds have been obtained and the purpose to which they have been put. A cash flow statement shows the receipts and payments of cash and is most commonly used as a management tool to budget for future cash requirements.

2 Statement of Source and Application of Funds

This is also known as a flow of funds statement and it forms part of the audited accounts of a limited company. It may deal with the source and application of any 'fund', for example:

(a)   Working capital, defined as current assets less current liabilities.

(b)   Cash.

(c)   Net liquid funds, that is cash and short-term investment less short-term borrowings.

(d)   Net liquid assets, that is cash, short-term investments, debtors and creditors. In practice the majority of firms produce a working capital flow statement, and a substantial minority produce a cash flow statement. However, in principle the published flow of funds statements refer not to the actual flow of funds, but to the annual profit made by the business. The purpose of a statement of the source and application of funds is to show the manner in which the operation is financed and how the financial resources are used. The information is simply a selection, reorganisation and reclassification of the figures in the profit and loss account and balance sheet. In order to show precisely the nature of the change in break-down between assets and liabilities, the statement should show as many individual figures as practicable and have the minimum of 'netting off'. Unfortunately, there is no standard governing this in 1980 and some firms do produce statements with important figures netted off against each other. Some information about this should be present in the profit and loss account and balance sheet and be revealed by close scrutiny.

Example

Funds flow statement of working capital reconciled to net profit.

The statement merely uses information given in the profit and loss account and balance sheet. The balance sheets for two years are shown side by side and an analysis is made of the change in the constituent parts.

Ernie Enterprise

Balance Sheet as at 31 December

	19x2	19x1	19x2	19x1	Analysis of changes
	£	£	£	£	£
Fixed Assets					
Freehold property			29,200	10,000	19,200
Plant and machinery			6,250	7,500	(1,250)
Motor vehicles			4,875	6,500	(1,625)
			40,325	24,000	
Current Assets					
Stock	25,000	22,000			3,000
Debtors	16,000	15,000			1,000
Cash	10,000	16,500			(6,500)
	51,000	53,500			
Less Current Liabilities					
Creditors	16,500	15,500			1,000
Net Working Capital			34,500	38,000	
Net Value of Assets			£74,825	£62,000	
Capital			54,825	52,000	2,825
Long-term loans			20,000	10,000	10,000
			£74,825	£62,000	

Ernie Enterprise
Profit and Loss Account
31 December 19x2

	£
Profit from operations	9,675
Less depreciation	3,675
Net profit for the year	6,000
Capital 1.1.19x2	52,000
	58,000
Proprietor's drawings	3,175
Capital 31.12.19x2	£54,825

Notes to the accounts
Fixed Assets

	Freehold property £	Plant and machinery £	Motor vehicles £	Total £
Cost				
At 1 Jan. 19x2	20,000	12,500	8,125	40,625
Additions	20,000	—	—	20,000
At 31 Dec. 19x2	40,000	12,500	8,125	60,625
Accumulated depreciation				
At 1 Jan. 19x2	10,000	5,000	1,625	16,625
Charges	800	1,250	1,625	3,675
At 31 Dec. 19x2	10,800	6,250	3,250	20,300
Net book value				
At 31 Dec. 19x2	29,200	6,250	4,875	40,325
At 31 Dec. 19x1	10,000	7,500	6,500	24,000

Statement of the Source and Application of Funds
31 December 19x2

	£	£
Source of funds		
Net profit		6,000
Depreciation		3,675
Total generated from operations		9,675
Funds from other sources		
Bank loan		10,000
		19,675
Application of funds		
Proprietor's drawings	(3,175)	
Purchase of fixed assets	(20,000)	
		(23,175)
		(3,500)

	£	£
Changes in working capital		
Increase in stock	3,000	
Increase in debtors	1,000	
Increase in creditors	(1,000)	
Movement in net liquid funds		
Decrease in cash balances	(6,500)	
		(3,500)

PRODUCTION OF THE STATEMENT

It will be clearly seen that the information in the statement of the source and application of funds is a selection of the information available in the profit and loss account and balance sheet. It should be understood that the note to the accounts on the cost and accumulated depreciation of the fixed assets is an integral part of the accounts.

The statement begins with the major source of funds, the net profit. This figure comes from the profit and loss account. It is necessary to add back depreciation to this, as depreciation is merely a book exercise in spreading, or amortising, the cost of fixed assets over their working life, and does not affect any actual flow of funds. When an asset is purchased the purchase price affects the flow of funds and this is dealt with later. Funds may be obtained from outside sources in the form of loans, debentures or share issues and these are shown next. The additional loan is revealed in the balance sheet.

Having analysed the source of funds, the statement deals with how these funds have been used. In this case, the proprietor has withdrawn cash from the business; in a limited company dividends may have been paid. Fixed assets have been purchased, and the cost of the new assets is shown in the note.

Comparison betweeen the source and application of funds reveals a deficit of £3,500, and this must mean a reduction in the working capital of the business. The changes in working capital are analysed next. An increase in stock and debtors necessitates additional working capital. This is obtained partly from an increase in creditors—these are effectively short-term borrowings—and partly from the reduction in cash balances, leaving an overall reduction of £3,500.

ANALYSIS OF THE STATEMENT

The major financial transaction during the year was the purchase of property for £20,000, and this has been financed by a bank loan of £10,000, the year's trading profits of £6,500, and the decrease in cash balances. These facts are emphasised by the presentation of the statement. The other point shown up is that the need for working capital is increasing, as the expansion of the business, or merely inflation, leads to a higher stock and debtor balances and a consequent decrease in the cash balances.

Example

Funds flow statement of cash reconciled to net profit. The figures on the statement can be re-sorted to show the effect of the year's trading on the cash balances.

Statement of the Source and Application of Funds

31 December 19x2

	£	£
Source of funds		
Net profit	6,000	
Depreciation	3,675	
		9,675
Bank loan		10,000
Increase in creditors		1,000
		20,675
Application of funds		
Proprietor's drawings	3,175	
Purchase of fixed assets	20,000	
Increase in stock	3,000	
Increase in debtors	1,000	
		(27,175)
Decrease in cash balances		(6,500)

There is a difference in emphasis between the two statements. The one relating to cash balances purports to show whence the money has come and whither it has gone. However, although this format is popular it must be noted that there is a considerable difference between profitability and liquidity. A business will not necessarily succeed just because it is profitable; it is essential to have sufficient finance available to pay one's immediate liabilities. Indeed, it sometimes happens that the very success of a business causes its downfall, in that it may expand too quickly and be unable to finance its increased requirement for working capital; it is then unable to pay its creditors and goes into liquidation. This syndrome is known as overtrading.

3   Cash Flow Statement

In order to avoid the pitfall of overtrading, it is sensible to budget for the future cash requirements, and this is done by means of a cash flow statement. It is done on a weekly or monthly basis since a satisfactory cash position at the beginning and end of a year may hide a shortfall in the middle.

To draw up a cash flow statement it is necessary to estimate future sales and expenses. This means that the cash flow is liable to error and may have to be updated in the light of experience. Nevertheless, it is a useful tool and can be instrumental in raising finance.

Example

Ernie Enterprise decided to draw up a cash flow statement for 19x3. He estimated that his sales would be £7,000 a month with additional sales of £4,000 a month from April to June, and that in 19x4 sales would increase to £8,000 a month with seasonal peaks of £12,000. All sales are on credit and debtors pay in the second month after delivery. Sales in the last two months of 19x2 were equal. Creditors are paid in the second month after delivery. Stock sufficient for four months' sales is kept on hand and the gross profit percentage is 25%.

Wages are a consistent £800 a month and overheads £200. Rent is £2,000 a year and is paid in equal instalments on the quarter-days. Ernie anticipates taking drawings of £4,500 in May.

Ernie has placed a contract for machinery costing £10,000 due to be delivered in June. Payment will be made in two equal instalments, the first on installation and the second three months later.

Workings

(a)   Debtors will pay for January's sales in March.

(b)   Purchases in January will be for stock necessary for sale in May, as four months stock is kept on hand. Sales in May are estimated at £11,000. The gross profit percentage is 25% so the cost of sales must be 75% of the selling price of £8,250. These goods will not be paid for until March.

(c)   The quarter-days fall in March, June, September and December.

Ernie's cash flow (p. 176) shows that he will require some short-term borrowing to cover the projected deficiency in June and July. A bank overdraft is probably most suited to his needs and he has plenty of time to arrange for this. Alternatively he may defer part of his drawings for a couple of months.

The purchase of the machinery is financed out of profits and cash balances, but note must be taken of the dwindling cash balance and the increased requirement for working capital. It is time that Ernie started to think of ways of raising additional finance.

It is because such matters are best arranged well in advance of requirements that many firms produce budgets and cash flows for five years ahead.

4   Summary

(a)   A statement of the source and application of funds may deal with any 'fund', but published accounts most commonly contain statements of the flow of working capital or cash.

(b)   It comprises a selection and reorganisation of figures in the profit and loss account and balance sheet.

(c)   The purpose of the funds flow statement is to show how the financial resources of the business are used.

(d)   A cash flow statement shows the receipts and payments of cash, and can be used to forecast future cash requirements.

Cash Flow 19x3

	Jan. £	Feb. £	March £	April £	May £	June £	July £	Aug. £	Sept. £	Oct. £	Nov. £	Dec. £
Inflows												
Opening cash b/f	10,000	9,200	7,900	5,350	3,300	(250)	(800)	4,150	9,100	4,550	5,500	5,700
Debtors receipts	8,000	8,000	7,000	7,000	7,000	11,000	11,000	11,000	7,000	7,000	7,000	7,000
Total	18,000	17,200	14,900	12,350	10,300	10,750	10,200	15,150	16,100	11,550	12,500	12,700
Outflows												
Payments to creditors	8,000	8,500	8,250	8,250	5,250	5,250	5,250	5,250	5,250	5,250	6,000	6,000
Wages	800	800	800	800	800	800	800	800	800	800	800	800
Rent			500			500			500			500
Machinery						5,000			5,000			
Drawings					4,500							
Total	8,800	9,300	9,550	9,050	10,550	11,550	6,050	6,050	11,550	6,050	6,800	7,300
Closing cash c/f	9,200	7,900	5,350	3,300	(250)	(800)	4,150	9,100	4,550	5,500	5,700	5,400

Questions

17.1 Hilary Haighton owns her own engineering business. She has studied statements of the source and application of funds in published accounts, and would like one for her own business. From the following draw up a statement of the source and application of funds relating to working capital:

Balance sheet
as at 31 December

	19XI	19X0	19XI	19X0
Fixed Assets	£	£	£	£
At cost Jan. 1			10,000	11,000
Additions			2,000	—
Disposals				(1,000)
At cost Dec. 31			12,000	10,000
Less depreciation			(6,200)	(5,000)
Net book value			5,800	5,000
Current Assets				
Stock	13,000	9,700		
Debtors	6,200	5,300		
Cash	2,000	2,500		
	21,200	17,500		
Current Liabilities				
Creditors	(6,000)	(5,000)		
Net working capital			15,200	12,500
Net value of assets			£21,000	£17,500
Capital			16,000	14,500
Long-term loans			5,000	3,000
Capital employed			£21,000	£17,500

Profit and Loss Account
31 December 19X1

	£
Trading profit	7,700
Less depreciation	(1,200)
Net profit for the year	6,500
Capital 1.1.19X1	14,500
	21,000
Less proprietor's drawings	(5,000)
Capital 31.12.19X1	£16,000

17.2 After receiving her fund flow statement relating to working capital, Hilary phones to inquire why some published funds flow statements analyse the change in cash balances. You promise to produce one for her in that format.

17.3 From the following accounts at Bangs Incorporated, manufacturers of fireworks, calculate the variation in working capital and explain how the variation has arisen by means of a statement of source and application of funds:

Balance Sheet

as at 31 December

	19X4 £	19X3 £	19X4 £	19X3 £
Fixed assets				
At cost Jan. 1			15,000	15,000
Additions			5,000	—
Disposals			(2,000)	—
At cost Dec. 31			18,000	15,000
Less depreciation			(7,000)	(6,000)
Net book value			11,000	9,000
Current Assets				
Stock	15,000	8,500		
Debtors	9,000	6,000		
Cash	500	5,000		
	24,500	19,500		
Current Liabilities				
Creditors	(7,000)	(6,500)		
Net working capital			17,500	13,000
Net value of assets			£28,500	£22,000
Capital			23,500	22,000
Long-term loans			5,000	—
Capital employed			£28,500	£22,000

Profit and Loss Account

31 December, 19X4

	£
Trading profit	9,500
Less depreciation	(1,800)
Less loss on the sale of fixed assets	(200)
Net profit for the year	7,500
Capital 1.1.x4	22,000
	29,500
Less proprietor's drawings	(6,000)
Capital 31.12.x4	£23,500

Note

Fixed assets were sold for £1,000 during 19x4.

17.4 The managing director of Bangs Incorporated was most interested in the statement of source and application of funds relating to working capital for 19x4. Nevertheless he was still perplexed as to why the bank balance had fallen so dramatically over the past year. 'We are making a profit and the new investment was entirely supported by a bank loan.' Demonstrate to Mr. Spark the whereabouts of the missing cash.

17.5 Willy Weedon, having failed to interest an established company in manufacturing his revolutionary new gardening tool, Weedit, is considering setting up in business on his own account.

(a) He has £10,000 to invest and can obtain an interest-free loan of £35,000.

(b) He will require machinery costing £10,000, payable in two equal instalments, the first on delivery and the other three months later. It will have an expected life of five years.

(c) Each 'Weedit' will require 500 grams of raw material costing £1, which will be purchased the month before it is required for production. In addition there will be a reserve stock of 200 kilos. In the first month of business it will be necessary to purchase stock for the first two months' production. Suppliers expect to be paid in the month of purchase.

(d) The wage rate is £2 an hour and each 'Weedit' takes one man-hour to complete. Wages are paid in the month in which they are incurred.

(e) When production starts there will be enough 'Weedits' made each month for the following month's sales. They will sell for £5 each and anticipated demand is as follows:

Month 2	4,000
Month 3 and subsequent	5,000

(f) Customers are allowed one month's credit, so debts should be paid the month after they are incurred.

(g) Other expenses will amount to £1,500 a month payable as incurred.

(h) Willy will withdraw £400 a month for his personal use.

    (i) Prepare Willy's budgeted cash flow for the first four months of business.

    (ii) Consider the profitability of manufacturing 'Weedits'.

Chapter 18   AVERAGES

In order to make comparisons between one group and another, it is necessary to have one figure that is representative of each group. This representative figure may be termed the 'average' of the group. There are several ways of calculating the 'average' and the method chosen will depend on which best represents the property of the group under discussion.

1   The Arithmetic Mean

This is the usual arithmetical average. It is calculated by adding the value of the items and dividing by the total number of items.

Example 1

A company's sales for six months were as follows:
£60,000, £65,000, £62,000, £66,000, £65,000, £63,000.
The total sales for the period were £381,000.
The period was 6 months.

$$\text{The arithmetic mean } = \frac{381,000}{6} = £63,500.$$

It should be noted that, although the figure of £63,500 is taken to be representative of the sales during the six-month period, yet in no month was £63,500 worth of goods actually sold.

Example 2

Over a five-week period a machine operator's take-home pay was as follows:
£80.40, £85.50, £94.60, £79.50, and £87.00.
His total take-home pay was £427.
The period was 5 weeks.

$$\text{The arithmetic mean } = \frac{427}{5} = £85.40.$$

Again it should be noted that he never took home £85·40 in any week.

Although the arithmetic mean is in common use, being simple to calculate and easy to understand, yet it can give a misleading result if one value is at an extreme.

Example 3

Salaries in a small company are as follows:

Managing Director	20,000
Accountant	8,500
Foreman	4,500
10 machinists each earn £3,500	35,000
	68,000

The arithmetic average $= \dfrac{68,000}{13} = £5,230.$

However, only two people out of the thirteen earn a salary above £5,230; the other eleven earn less. The average has been distorted by the exceptionally high managing director's salary.

2   The Median

To overcome this distortion another method of finding a representative figure may be used. To find the median the items are arranged in order of size, and the middle item is the median. If there are an even number of items the simple average of the middle two may be taken to give the median.

Example 4

Using Example 3, the salaries arranged in order of size are:

20,000, 8,500, 4,500, 3,500, 3,500, 3,500, 3,500, 3,500, 3,500, 3,500, 3,500, 3,500, 3,500.

The median is the seventh item which is £3,500. This gives a more representative picture of the amount that the employees earn, but it gives little indication of the amount the company expends on salaries.

Example 5

A company's sales for six months arranged in order of size were:
£60,000, £62,000, £63,000, £65,000, £65,000, £66,000.

The middle figures are the third and fourth; a simple average of these is

$\dfrac{63,000 + 65,000}{2} = £64,000$ which is the median.

This is the same as Example 1. The arithmetic mean is £63,500. The figures are close and this indicates that both give a fair representation of the sales.

The advantage of the median as a representative of average is that it mitigates the effects of extreme values, as can be seen in the fourth example. It is also useful when the exact values of extreme data are unknown.

Example 6
Heights of women from a random sample in a given area

Height	Under 5'2"	5'2"	5'3"	5'4"	5'5"	5'6"	5'7"	5'8"	over 5'8"
Number	242	83	84	85	80	60	54	49	88

There are 825 women in the sample. The median is the 413th item and this lies in the group of women who are 5'4". The median height of the sample is 5'4".

It would be difficult to calculate the arithmetic mean of this sample, owing to the indefinite data at the two extremes.

3   The Mode

This is the most frequent value which occurs in a given set of data. This means that the mode is the most typical or popular value. As such it is often used to represent the average family size, or the average income. The arithmetic mean and the median may represent values which actually occur in the data, but the mode definitely does. The mode is a most useful figure for planning. It is not very sensible to build houses to suit the 'average' family with 2·5 children. What are required are houses for the spectrum of family sizes from one upwards.

Example 7
The output of Widgets on ten consecutive days was as follows:

    60, 65, 70, 75, 80, 80, 75, 70, 60, 60.

On three days 60 widgets were produced.
On two days 70, 75 and 80 widgets were produced.
On one day 65 widgets were produced.
The mode for the output of widgets is 60.
This figure can be compared with the arithmetic mean which is 69·5 widgets, and the median which is 70.

Example 8
The following figures on family size were obtained from a random sample taken in a given area.

Family size.							
No. of persons.	1	2	3	4	5	6	over 6
No. of families.	6	19	17	31	14	9	4

The modal family comprises 4 persons. However, such a sample can give an indication of the quantities of housing required to suit each family size.

The arithmetic mean would be difficult to calculate owing to the uncertainty of the data at the extreme range. The median is between the 50th and the 51st item both of which lie in the family of 4 persons.

In practice the mode is usually found for large quantities of data, so there is little chance of there being more than one mode in any set of data. However, this can occur and the mode is only satisfactory as a representative figure of a set of data when there is only one mode.

4 The Weighted Average

Example 9

A business purchased the following items of stock:

1500 units at £3.70
2000 units at £3.90
3000 units at £4.00

What was the average price paid?

In total:

$$
\begin{array}{rcl}
1,500 \text{ at } 3.70 &=& 5,550 \\
2,000 \text{ at } 3.90 &=& 7,800 \\
3,000 \text{ at } 4.00 &=& 12,000 \\
\hline
6,500 & & 25,350
\end{array}
$$

6,500 units cost 25,350 so the average price per unit was $\dfrac{25,350}{6,500} = £3.90$.

Note the average of the prices paid is $\dfrac{3.70 + 3.90 + 4.00}{3} = £3.86$

but this is NOT the average price per unit.

Example 10

A jewellers' firm bought gold at various prices throughout the month:

$$
\begin{array}{rcl}
1,200 \text{ ounces at } £370 &=& £444,000 \\
1,000 \text{ ounces at } £379.40 &=& £379,400 \\
500 \text{ ounces at } £410 &=& £205,000 \\
2,000 \text{ ounces at } £360 &=& £720,000 \\
\hline
4,700 & & £1,748,400
\end{array}
$$

The average price the firm paid for gold during the month was

$$\frac{1,748,400}{4,700} = £372 \text{ per ounce.}$$

Questions

18.1 Calculate the arithmetic mean of the following:

£367, £425, £793, £211, £914, £105.

18.2 Town population	50,000	75,000	100,000	150,000
No. of towns	8	14	17	11

Calculate the arithmetic mean of the town population.

18.3

Salary	£4,000	£4,500	£5,000	£6,000	£8,000
No. of employees	500	300	100	50	5

Calculate the arithmetic mean of the employees' salaries. Find the median salary.

18.4 The mean of a set of six figures is 8·5; the mean of a different set of eight figures is 7·25. Calculate the mean of the combined set of fourteen figures.

18.5 A golfer wants to average 5 shots a hole over an 18-hole golf course. He is ready to tee off on the final hole and has already taken 87 shots. How many more shots can he take and still achieve his average?

18.6 A saleswoman is entitled to an annual bonus if she averages a monthly sales figure of £2,000. During the last eleven months she has made sales worth £20,750. How many items valued at £3·25 must she sell during December to receive her bonus?

18.7 A company manufactures and sells one product, wotsits. Owing to an unprecedented increase in the cost of raw materials and labour, it is forced to raise its selling price by 20% on July 1 and by a further 10% on October 1. The selling price at the beginning of the year, January 1, was £5·50.
The monthly sales figures for the year follow:

Jan.	Feb.	March	April	May	June	July	Aug.	Sept.	Oct.	Nov.	Dec.
1,000	1,100	1,050	1,150	1,250	1,400	1,500	1,500	1,300	1,100	1,000	1,000

Calculate the average selling price of a wotsit during the year.

18.8 Locate the median in the following sets of data:
(a) 94, 87, 21, 43, 79, 32, 54.
(b) 17, 46, 97, 23, 85, 63, 34, 22.
(c) 1, ·02, ·006, ·015, ·6, ·008, ·07.

18.9 Find the mode in the following sets of data.
(a) 5, 7, 5, 8, 9, 3, 5, 3, 3, 6, 1, 4, 5, 2, 6, 9.
(b) 39%, 42%, 89%, 65%, 73%, 45%, 42%, 43%, 42%, 54%, 55%.

18.10 Find the modal shirt size from the following sales figures.

Shirt size.	14½	15	15½	16	16½	17
No. sold	56	65	90	45	30	15

18.11 In a certain week company employees earn the following sums:
10 earn £60, 35 earn £100, 25 earn £200 and 30 earn £300.
(a) Find the mean, median and mode of this wage distribution.
(b) Which of these will be altered, and by how much, if 4 people work overtime and each increases his earnings by £50?

18.12 The figures show the sales of 50 representatives:

Sales	£150	£200	£250	£300	£350	£650
No. of reps.	5	12	15	13	4	1

(a) Find the mean, median and mode of this sales distribution.
(b) Calculate the arithmetic mean ignoring the salesman with the highest figure.

18.13 A factory manufactures thingummybobs; the production for 10 consecutive working days is as follows:
64, 40, 40, 53, 56, 74, 69, 69, 71, 69.
(a) Find the mean and the median output.
(b) Which do you think gives the fairer representation of the factory's production?

18.14 Sam Smart wants to start a small business; he requires an income of £8,500 p.a. and estimates his overheads will be £6,500 p.a. He will have a ready market for sales of £1,000 a week over a fifty-week year. What ratio of gross profit to sales must he achieve in order to realise his required income?

Chapter 19 ELEMENTARY CORRELATION

1 Discrete and Continuous Variables

In order to draw logical conclusions about a given situation it is necessary to collect information, or data. This data will give facts about the variable characteristics of the situation under review. These variable characteristics fall into two groups; those which can take only certain definite values, discrete variables; and those which may take any value within a given range, continuous variables.

(a) DISCRETE DATA

A collection of variables which take definite values. For example:
  (i)   The marks obtained by a class in their last accountancy examination.
  (ii) The number of Minis sold each week by British Leyland.
  (iii) The number of aircraft movements from London Heathrow on a particular day.

Examination marks are usually given as a whole number expressed as a percentage; they may take any of the values between 0 and 100 but no intermediate values. Minis are only sold as complete units, and fractions of aeroplanes are incapable of flight.

(b) CONTINUOUS DATA

A collection of variables which may take any values within a given range. For example:
  (i)   The distance travelled by a car from rest until it stops.
  (ii) The production of chemicals at a chemical plant.
  (iii) The height of students on a Business Studies course.

A car can travel any distance from a fraction of an inch to many hundreds of miles. Any quantity of chemicals may be produced from tonnes to fractions of a gram. Individual heights may differ by indiscernible amounts.

186

It is important to differentiate between discrete and continuous data as the method of dividing the data into sub-classes is different. With a large quantity of data it is necessary to divide it into classes in order to tabulate it. With discrete data the division is straightforward, but with continuous data it may be difficult to decide whether a given quantity is slightly greater or smaller than some arbitrary figure. In this case it is essential that the intervals for division are closed at one end and open at the other. For example: 200 tonnes but less than 300 tonnes; 300 tonnes but less than 400 tonnes; and so on. In this way one ensures that no item is omitted or included twice.

2   Dependent and Independent Variables

Once the data on a situation has been collected, divided into classes and tabulated, the researcher will wish to see if there are causal relationships between any of the variables. A great deal of data is required to establish a causal relationship, and there is considerable scope for error. Consider an instance when the telephone rings and the washing-machine, which has lain silent for the past five minutes, promptly starts to spin. It may be thought that the bell was a signal for the washing machine to continue its programme, but it would require a great number of tests to determine whether this were so, and it appears unlikely.

On the other hand, it does not require a great amount of information to establish that variables are related in some degree, although not necessarily causally connected. Consider the instance when one clock points to four o'clock, and another clock chimes the hour. The two happenings are not causally related, in that the movement of the first clock did not cause the second to strike, but both are connected to a third factor, namely the time of day.

Variables are said to be correlated if they behave in such a way that changes in the value of one variable enable changes in the value of the other variable to be predicted.

When a causal relationship has been established, the variable which may be considered the 'prime mover' in the relationship is termed the *independent variable*, and the variable which is altered by a change in this first variable is termed the *dependent variable*.

In practice it can be extremely difficult to determine which variable is independent and which dependent. Consider the following situation. A company raises its prices but this reduces demand, therefore the reduced demand forces the company to lower its prices. In the first instance price is the independent variable and demand the dependent; but in a short while the situation is reversed and demand becomes the independent variable and price the dependent.

Another instance where difficulties may arise is in the relationship between cost and volume of production. These are obviously causally connected, but is cost dependent on production, or is production dependent on cost? There is no correct answer; it depends from which angle the situation is being viewed.

Dependent and independent variables can be plotted on graphs to show their causal relationship, and this is dealt with in Chapter 20. However, variables which may or may not have a degree of correlation can be plotted on scatter diagrams in an attempt to discover whether there is indeed any correlation.

3   Scatter Diagrams

As its name suggests, a scatter diagram shows points representing collected data on a graph. These can then be studied visually to see whether there is any correlation between them.

Example 1

Store	1	2	3	4	5	6	7	8	9	10
Sales £'000	50	74	93	55	67	110	99	83	52	68
Profit £'000	5	10	18·5	8	8	20	11	11·5	9	13

The profit is dependent on the turnover, so the independent variable, the sales, is plotted along the horizontal or x axis, and the dependent variable, profit, along the vertical or y axis. A point is entered on the diagram for each of the stores.

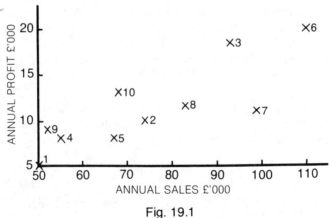

Fig. 19.1

The scales on a scatter diagram need not start from zero, as one is concerned only with the position of the points relative to one another.

It is now necessary to study the points to see whether there is any correlation. There seems to be a general upwards trend, which is marked by the extremes of stores 1 and 6, which are in a direct line with one another. A line of 'best fit' can be drawn. This is a straight line which is fitted visually to pass close to the maximum number of points. There should be approximately the same number of points left above as below the line, which is known technically as the regression line.

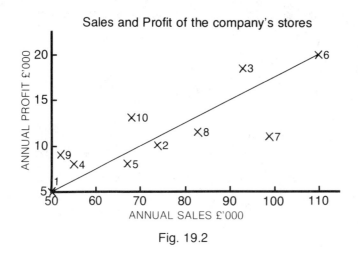

Fig. 19.2

The points are placed roughly along the line, so there is *linear correlation* between them, and it appears that as sales increase so do profits; this is called *positive correlation*.

Studying the diagram, it is possible to ascertain details of the relationships between the stores. The line of best fit shows not merely that profits increase with turnover, as is to be expected, but that the stores with higher turnover make a greater profit proportionately. Store 1 made a profit of £5,000 on sales of £50,000, which is a ten per cent return on sales, while store 6 made a profit of £20,000 on sales of £110,000 which is an 18% return on sales.

Stores 1 and 6 represent the average performance; the stores above the line of best fit, numbers 3, 4, 9, and 10, performed better than average. These stores may be studied to see what factors govern their success. The stores below the line of best fit performed less well, although numbers 2, 5, and 8 lie close to the line and so are close to average performance. Store 7 lies well below the line and the company management will have to decide how its performance can be improved.

Example 2
In Ruritania data has been collected concerning interest rates and the amount of investment in industry, covering the last ten years. Some economists believe that the

two figures may be linked. The information is tabulated below:

Interest rate %	5	7½	10	12½	15	17½	20	22½	25
Industrial investment £ millions	77	71	68	53	50	35	30	28.	15

It is believed that the level of investment may be dependent on the prevailing interest rate. Therefore, the interest rate is treated as the independent variable on the *x* axis, and the investment as the dependent variable on the *y* axis.

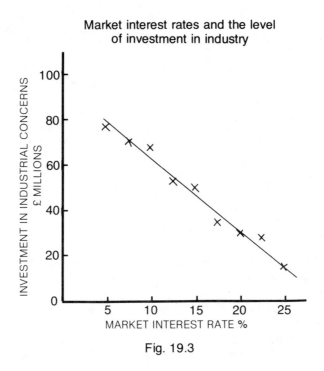

Market interest rates and the level of investment in industry

Fig. 19.3

The points are clustered closely to the line, so there is strong *linear correlation*. It does indeed appear that investment in industry decreases as interest rates rise; this is called *negative correlation*.

It might be expected that investment in industry would decrease as interest rates rise. If it is possible to obtain a high return on investment in the money market, where there is no risk, there is little point in risking capital in speculative industry, where the return is uncertain.

Example 3

Professor Bunce the well-known Ruritanian economist believes that when the level of unemployment rises there is a fall in average 'take-home' pay. Data has been collected concerning this, and figures taken from the last fifty years are tabulated below. Inflation has mercifully been very low in Ruritania during this period.

Unemployment millions.	·75	1	1·25	1·3	1·5	1·6	1·8	1·9	2·2	2·5
Weekly take-home pay £	44	60	36	45	68	27	35	55	38	31

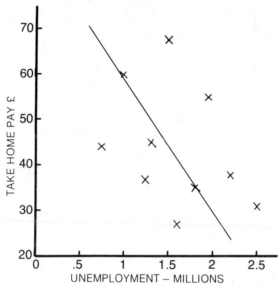

Level of unemployment and average take-home pay

Fig. 19.4

The points are scattered fairly widely, although there does appear to be a negative trend. There would appear to be some connection between unemployment and take-home pay, but the *correlation* is *weak*. The professor's theory seemed reasonable, but the diagram shows that the relationship is far from clear cut. It is possible that other factors should be taken into account such as substantial earnings related unemployment benefits, and a high rate of taxation.

Example 4
Professor Bunce wished to explore the possibility that wages might be forced higher through increased interest rates. The relevant data was extracted from the Ruritanian archives for the past ten years and tabulated overleaf.

Interest rate %	$2\frac{1}{2}$	5	$7\frac{1}{2}$	10	$12\frac{1}{2}$	15	$17\frac{1}{2}$	20	$22\frac{1}{2}$	25
Weekly take-home pay £		25	78	35	55	41	45	35	66	30	60

Market interest rates and average take-home pay

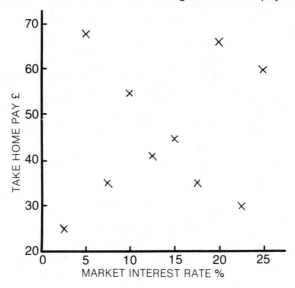

Fig. 19.5

The points are scattered all over the graph; there appears to be no correlation at all between the data.

It should be noted that genuine scatter diagrams are used to correlate large samples of data, and are not suitable for plotting small amounts such as have been used in the above examples. It is not practical to give examples with a hundred points or more, and the principles can be explained more easily with small samples.

However, genuine scatter diagrams are more difficult to interpret for this reason, and the results must be treated with great caution. Not only can it be difficult to perceive trends, but there is always a danger that a researcher may twist the facts to fit his own theories. Occasionally, scatter diagrams have been published with the line of best fit featuring prominently, and the points omitted entirely. Such a diagram is most misleading.

With all statistical work the diagrams, graphs and hence the conclusions are only as good as the basic data. If the accounts are incorrect, it will be impossible to draw sound conclusions from them. If a general survey of business is being conducted it is essential that the sample chosen is representative, and not biased towards one regional area, type or size of firm.

Statistics can be a valuable aid in decision-making, but all data, results and conclusions must be examined with great care, to ensure that the ensuing management decisions are soundly based.

Questions

19.1 Define and differentiate between discrete and continuous data.

19.2 Differentiate between dependent and independent variables.

19.3 What problems may arise when determining which variables are independent and which dependent?

19.4 Plot the following data on a scatter diagram, draw a line of best fit, and state what type of correlation you can see.

Year	1	2	3	4	5	6	7	8	9	10
Advertising expenditure £'000	54	59	82	78	87	90	71	65	91	93
Net profit £ million	·7	·62	·65	·73	·8	·97	·81	·88	·9	·98

19.5 A company which owns a chain of shoe shops has discovered from the annual returns from the branches that there are considerable differences in the rent paid for premises. The management wish to know whether there is any correlation between turnover and rent paid. Plot a scatter diagram from the following data and report your findings to the managing director:

Shop	1	2	3	4	5	6	7	8	9	10
Rent £'000	3	10	5	14	17	22	20	7·5	24	2·5
Sales £'000	120	106	88	83	61	118	63	60	120	60

19.6 The managing director and major shareholder of a small private company seeks your advice. He wishes to continue trading, but for the business to remain viable prices must be increased considerably. However, he fears that a price increase will lead to a drop in sales, as there have been several price increases in recent months. He tried reducing his prices two years ago, but was unable to quantify the results. To make a decision he requires to know the effect of previous price increases. Plot the information given on a scatter diagram, and make any suitable comments.

Sales price per unit £	51	54	57	62	69	73	78	84	90	92
Units sold '000	14	16	17·5	17	19·5	18	19	15·5	17	14

Chapter 20 GRAPHS

1 Uses of Graphs in Statistics

A graph is a pictorial representation of data. Although the data may be of a technical nature, trends can more easily be spotted on a graph than in pages of figures. When graphs do reveal trends, it may be possible to interpolate intermediate values of a variable. Finally, graphs may show correlations between variables.

2 Direct Proportion Graphs

(a) If two variables are directly proportionate, the graph will be represented as a straight line.

Example 1
£1 is equivalent to $2 US. Draw a graph to illustrate this with values ranging up to £50. Show on the graph the dollar equivalent of £24.

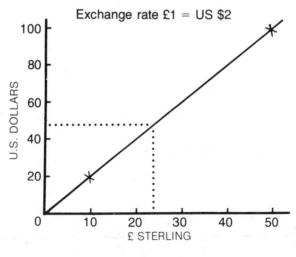

Fig. 20.1

Two points can be obtained by calculation and marked with crosses:

$£10 = US \$20$
$£50 = US \$100$

A line can then be drawn to connect the points. The graph can be used to show the dollar equivalent of the sterling values. A dotted line is drawn from the £24 on the x axis to the line. At the point where the two intersect a dotted line can be drawn to the y axis and the value of dollars read. So £24 = US $48.

(b)   If one variable is directly proportionate to the square of another, the graph will be presented as a smooth curve.

Example 2
Draw a graph of the function $x = y^2$ with values of x ranging up to 80. Show the value of y when x equals 44 on the graph.

When x equals 44, y equals between 1,900 and 1,950. This shows one of the drawbacks of graphs; although they give immediate visual impact they are not as accurate for discovering intermediate variables as is calculation. 44 squared is 1,936. However, they are extremely useful for estimating intermediate variables when there is insufficient data to perform a calculation.

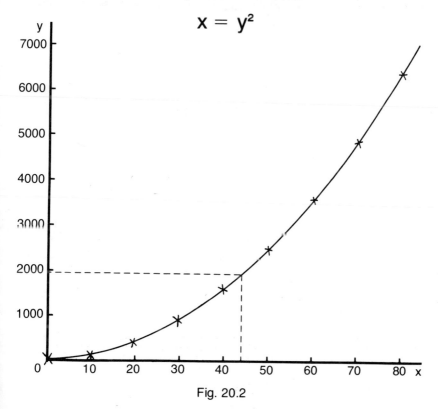

Fig. 20.2

3   Graphs Plotted from Collected Data

Many graphs plotted from collected data will have time as the independent variable, and these are known as historigrams, as they give information on past history. It is rarely possible to draw the graphs as either a straight line or a smooth curve, since life tends to be more erratic than algebraic functions.

Example 3
Draw a graph to show the following information:

Monthly sales during the last 2 years (£'000)

Year	Jan.	Feb.	March	April	May	June	July	Aug.	Sept.	Oct.	Nov.	Dec.
19X1	19	18	22	30	39	55	50	50	44	30	22	20
19X2	20	21	21	25	48	61	58	57	46	30	21	21

The graph portrays dramatically the peak sales during the summer months and the doldrums of the winter. Nevertheless, there seems to be a slight overall increase in sales, as the second half of the graph representing 19x2 is a little higher than the portion representing 19x1.

The company sells garden furniture in Britain. Sales are low during the cold winter months and begin to improve with the spring in April and May rising to a peak in June. Low sales could be expected in a wet spring, but a hot or prolonged summer should cause increased sales.

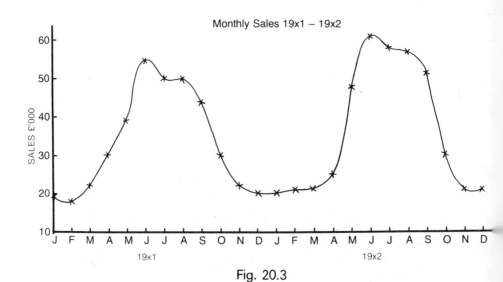

Fig. 20.3

Example 4

Sometimes the data is composed of average rather than actual figures. The following table shows the average weekly production of sugar month by month:

Weekly average production of sugar 19x3 (thousand tonnes)

Jan.	Feb.	March	April	May	June	July	Aug.	Sept.	Oct.	Nov.	Dec.
45	38	54	55	48	45	39	37	46	51	53	49

As the figures are averages they are plotted at the mid-point of the period which they represent. No point between the plotted points has any meaning, so no smooth curve is drawn between the points. A smooth curve indicates that the intermediate variables can be taken with reasonable accuracy.

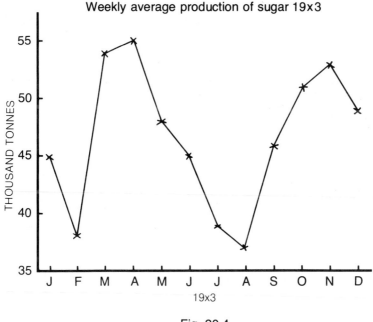

Fig. 20.1

Production seems to be low in February, which suffers not only from being a short month, but also, in northern climes, from a considerable amount of absenteeism through sickness. From there production rises, as people are eager to do overtime to save for their summer holiday. In May holidays begin to be taken, and production falls to a low in August which is the main European holiday season. Production rises again in September as workers return, and continues to rise in anticipation of the Christmas bonus.

4 Ratio graphs

The graphs drawn so far are all on absolute scales; no allowance has been made for relative change. When considering certain aspects of a business it can be most useful to consider the relative improvement or failure. For example, the percentage increase in turnover may well be a more relevant figure to consider than the absolute.

In order to show relative change only one axis, the y axis, is measured in the ratio scale. Such graphs are known as semi-logarithmic graphs. It is possible to draw full logarithmic graphs with both axes on a ratio scale but this is usually done in scientific work rather than in the world of finance.

Ratio graphs need a little more care in interpretation. The most important feature in a ratio graph is the degree of slope at any point. Equal distances on a ratio scale always show equal percentage change, but the distances are not directly proportionate to one another. That is, a fifty per cent increase will *not* be twice the distance of a twenty-five per cent increase, and this can cause some confusion in interpretation.

Example 5
The sales figures for a company for the past five years follow:

Year	19X1	19X2	19X3	19X4	19X5
Sales £'000	20	40	60	80	100
(Logs. of) Sales	4·3010	4·6021	4·7782	4·9031	5

The sales are to be plotted on a ratio or logarithmic scale. First, the logarithms for the sales figures must be looked up in tables. Logarithms express a number as a power of ten. Powers are dealt with in Chapter 2. Any number which is at least 10 but less than 100 will have a 1 before the decimal point, as 10 is only one 10. Any number which is at least 100 but less than 1,000 will have a 2 before the decimal point, as 100 is 10^2, and so on. The numbers 20,000 to 80,000 lie between 10,000 and 100,000 and so will have 4 before the decimal point; 100,000 is 10^5. Look at Fig. 20.5.

The graph shows clearly that the increase in sales is flattening off. The increase in sales between 19X1 and 19X2 was 100%, but it took a further two years from 19X2 to 19X4 to obtain a further 100% increase. It can be seen on the y axis that the distance between £20,000 and £40,000 is equal to the distance between £40,000 and £80,000, both of which represent a hundred per cent increase. However, the distance between £40,000 and £60,000, which represents a 50% increase, is rather more than half the distance from £20,000 to £40,000.

This point is being laboured as the eye expects to see 50% as half of 100%, although it is plainly impossible for the same scale to show equal distances with an equal percentage change, and distances directly proportionate to one another. The

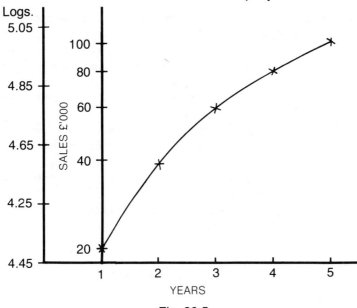

Fig. 20.5

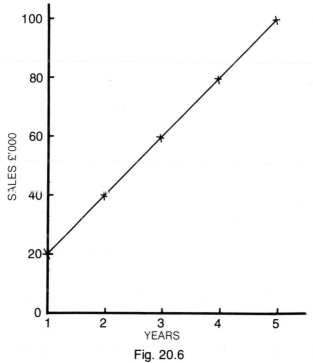

Fig. 20.6

two are mutually exclusive. It is possible to purchase semi-logarithmic graph paper, which is squared in ever narrowing bands, and avoids the need to actually calculate the logarithms of the figures to be plotted. It should be noted that there is no nought on the logarithmic scale. This is because the logarithm of one is nought and the logarithm of nought is minus infinity. The advantages of using the ratio scale can be seen when Fig 20.5. is compared with an absolute scale graph presenting the same information. Look at Fig. 20.6.

On the absolute graph the sales appear to have increased at a constant rate, while the ratio graph shows that this is not so and that performance, far from being consistent, is slackening. This interpretation must be treated with care, as a young business may expand rapidly in the early years as it finds a ready market. Later it may have to search further afield to find new markets.

Ratio graphs can be used to compare the performance of firms of differing sizes, and of firms and the industry average.

Example 6

During a trade recession the management of a small engineering firm survey the fall in sales gloomily. They wonder whether they are managing as well as other engineering firms, or the industry generally. They have the figures for the total industry sales from their trade journal, but find it difficult to compare them with their own.

Year	19X3	19X4	19X5	19X6	19X7
Firm's sales £'000	50	51	49	47	45
Industry sales £m	210	212	160	130	120

A ratio graph shows the following:

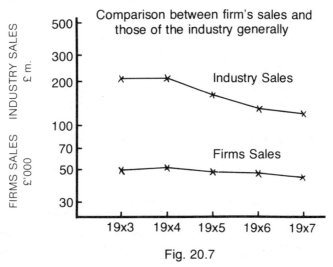

Fig. 20.7

It can be seen from the graph that while the firm's sales have dropped, they are not performing as badly as the industry generally.

Another use for a ratio graph is to look at price increases. Prices can appear to be rising rapidly on an absolute scale, but are not necessarily doing so on a relative scale.

Example 7
Widgets were invented in 19x5. The price then was £50. The prices in the following years were:

19x6	19x7	19x8	19x9
£75	£100	£130	£180

These can be represented on both absolute and ratio graphs (see Figs. 20.8 and 20.9).

From the absolute graph it appears that the price of widgets has been increasing more rapidly in recent years. However, the ratio graph shows that, to the contrary, the relative rate of price increase is slowing down.

It can be seen that it requires practice to interpret ratio graphs properly. However, there are considerable advantages in using them. Not only do they show the relative changes, but it is also possible to plot graphs of entirely different types on the same grid and using the same scale. For example, how can the size of a firm be measured? Should it be on turnover, on number of employees, on number of offices or branches, or might the profits be a better measurement? Obviously all these factors play a part in determining growth.

It would be difficult, if not impossible to plot all these factors on an absolute graph, as entirely different units are being measured—people, offices and money, Fortunately, it is possible to do so on a ratio scale graph as the basis of comparison is the rate of change.

5 Hints on Drawing Graphs

(a)   Look at figures and select a suitable scale. The aim is to have as large a scale as possible, and to try to be able to plot points where lines intersect.
(b)   Decide which factor is the independent variable, and mark the scale along the horizontal x axis. Name the axis. Mark the dependent variable along the vertical y axis. Name the axis. Ensure that the scales are shown for both variables.
(c)   Plot the points carefully.
(d)   Join the points, using a ruler if they fall along a straight line or a curve if they do not.
(e)   Mark any point you are required to read from the graph and join with dotted lines to both axes.
(f)   If necessary name the lines you have drawn.
(g)   Head the graph with an appropriate title.
(h)   Graphs cannot be as accurate as direct calculation but errors can be reduced by the use of a sharp, hard pencil and a firm smooth surface for drawing on.

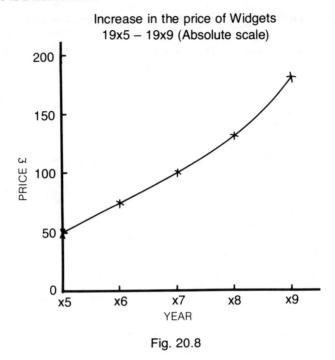

Fig. 20.8

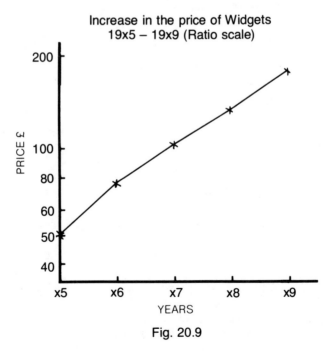

Fig. 20.9

6   Uses of Graphs

Many of the graphs produced for business purposes have more than one line plotted on them for purposes of comparison. These lines can be differentiated by colour, or by types of line, for example: thin, thick, dotted, dashed, and herring-bone. The scale on multi-line absolute graphs should start at zero to avoid being misleading.

Multi-line graphs can be used to compare many features of business finance. For example, a graph showing the monthly production, sales and profits could show the pattern throughout the year, and the delay between peak production and peak selling periods. A graph could be used to compare actual performance with that which was budgeted, or to show the comparative performance between one sales area or manager and another.

While ratio graphs are used for presenting business statistics, they are still considered to be rather technical. There is another simple method of showing relativity on an absolute scale graph which is found frequently. The method is to show the figures on the y axis as a proportion of the figures on the x axis. This can only be used when the two variables are related to each other, but is useful for showing such factors as the return on capital and the return on sales.

Example 8

Using the information given in Example 1 of Chapter 19, from which were derived Figs. 19.1 and 19.2, profit can be given as a percentage of sales thus:

Shop	1	2	3	4	5	6	7	8	9	10
Sales £'000	50	74	93	55	67	110	99	83	52	68
Profit £'000	5	10	18·5	8	8	20	11	11·5	9	13
% return on sales	10	13	20	15	12	18	11	14	17	19

Return on sales of 10 stores

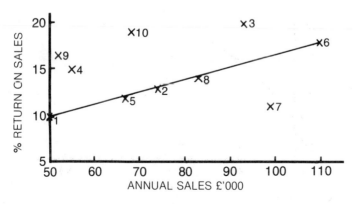

Fig. 20.10

The relationship between the points has altered slightly from the original diagrams. Shops numbers 5, 2 and 8 have moved closer to the line of best fit. It can be seen that although store 7 was considered to have below average performance for its size, yet its return on sales is actually greater than the return of store 1, which was considered average. Store 3 stands out as having the best return, but it is followed closely by store 10.

Questions

20.1 A woman is paid £49 for 35 hours' work. Assuming she is paid at a constant rate, draw a straight line graph to determine her pay for:
(a)   25 hours' work
(b)   39 hours' work.
How long would she have to work to earn:
(c)   £63?
(d)   £71·40?

20.2 At the current exchange rate £1 = 550 yen. Draw a graph to show the relationship between the British and Japanese currencies. Calculate from the graph:
(a)   The value in pounds of 13,750 yen.
(b)   The value in yen of £80.

20.3 There is a direct relationship between production and the cost of production, which can be expressed by the formula $5x + 5,000 = £y$, when x represents the units produced, and y the cost of production.
Draw a graph to show the cost of production up to 5000 units.

20.4 The following table shows sales of electric blankets throughout two consecutive years. Draw a graph to illustrate this.

Sales £'000

	Jan.	Feb.	March	April	May	June	July	Aug.	Sept.	Oct.	Nov.	Dec.
19X1	61	58	60	45	30	18	15	13	35	53	59	75
19X2	64	57	60	51	29	19	14	16	22	61	67	79

Comment on the pattern of sales revealed by your graph.

20.5 Represent graphically the following information:

Weekly average production of chemical ZX 9 19X5
Thousand tonnes

Jan.	Feb.	March	April	May	June	July	Aug.	Sept.	Oct.	Nov.	Dec.
101	89	105	112	116	120	93	87	99	113	108	105

Comment on the pattern of production revealed by your graph.

20.6 What are the main differences between an absolute scale and a ratio scale graph?
For what purposes are ratio scale graphs used?

20.7 Study the following graph showing the growth of Enterprise Ltd. for the eight years since its incorporation in 19x1. Taking each item individually, comment on the change in manpower, sales and profits. Then give a summary of the overall picture.

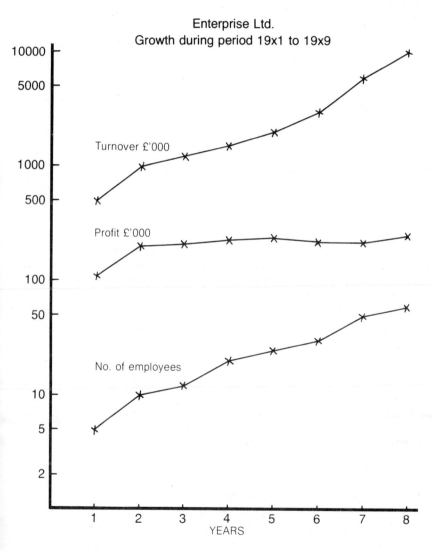

Enterprise Ltd.
Growth during period 19x1 to 19x9

Chapter 21   DIAGRAMS AND CHARTS

1   Tabulation of Data

Tabulation of data is an exercise in logic and clear thinking. It falls into two stages: classifying the data into groups, and then constructing a table suitable for portraying the information.

(a)   CLASSIFICATION

Raw data collected from surveys contains information both on characteristics which can be quantified and which are measurable, and on characteristics which cannot readily be measured such as colour and disease. The latter are termed attributes, and it usually requires a considerable knowledge of the subject-matter to classify them correctly.

Measurable characteristics are termed variables. They may be either discrete or continuous, and some will be dependent on other characteristics. The meaning of these terms is considered in detail in Chapter 19.

The data must be divided into classes which are both mutually exclusive and collectively exhaustive. For example: a collection of children's building blocks was classified according to whether the blocks were red, thick, or neither red nor thick. The group which was neither red nor thick excluded the other groups, but the group of red bricks, and the group of thick bricks contained some bricks which were both thick and red. It was necessary to have four classes:

> Blocks which were thick and red.
> Blocks which were thick but not red.
> Blocks which were red but not thick.
> Blocks which were neither thick nor red.

All the blocks are contained within these four classes; they are collectively exhaustive. No block will fall into more than one class, so the classes are mutually exclusive.

(b) TABULATION

The purpose of tabulation is to present classified data in a concise form, so that it can be studied easily and relationships noted. It is also easier to draw diagrams from neatly tabulated material.

i *Time Series* The simplest form of tabulation is that of a time series, which is a record of how a variable has changed in value over a period of time. Some of the graphs in Chapter 20 are drawn from examples of this kind of table.

ii *Space Series* This records changes in a variable in different geographical locations, for example in different countries, towns, sales areas or departments.

Example 1

Sales of Widgets and Boggits during 19x2

Region	Widgets £'000	Boggits £'000	Total £'000
Scotland	10	100	110
North East	75	50	125
North West	105	20	125
Midlands	100	10	110
Wales	25	5	30
London	115	35	150
South West	70	30	100
	500	250	750

The table shows clearly that there is twice the value of sales of widgets as of boggits, but that this pattern is by no means repeated from region to region.

The Scots appear to have a great penchant for boggits, as they purchase 40 % of the total sold, while buying only 14.67 % of total sales of both products.

Few sales are made in Wales; it may be that the product does not appeal to Welsh tastes, or perhaps there are few sales outlets.

The other areas seem comparable in size.

To interpret the table more fully, further information is required: a map showing the regions would be helpful, together with details of population and number of salesmen and sales outlets.

iii *Frequency tables*
Example 2
The managing director of a small company was worried as there seemed to have been a high rate of absence for sickness during the previous six months. Unfortunately, this coincided with the production of a new chemical XY7.

One hundred employees of both sexes were engaged on production and personal records showed that eighty of them had had at least one day's sickness during the previous 128 working days. The personnel manager produced the following data:

No. of days sickness for individual workers
during 128 working days 1.10.x6–31.3.x7

53	21	6	I	I	I	11	2	2	46	22	5	4	5	10	15
I	8	9	9	49	16	3	3	4	17	42	I	I	I	5	5
5	5	10	10	36	16	I	I	13	27	6	7	8	12	2	2
10	5	3	3	19	6	10	11	33	2	I	8	8	5	12	6
3	5	5	2	2	I	I	8	37	34	3	6	5	5	39	3

This raw data is not very informative as it stands; it needs to be organised to enable us to see if a pattern emerges. One method of organisation is to arrange the figures in numerical order; this is called an array:
I I I I I I I I I I I I 2 2 2 2 2 2 2 2 3 3 3 3 3 3 3 3 4 4, and so on.
This method is tedious, and not particularly easy to read. An improvement would be made by use of a simple frequency table.

No. of days' sickness: 1.10.x6–31.3.x7

No. of days absent	No. of absentees
I	12
2	7
3	7
4	2
5	12
6	5
7	I
8	5
9	2
10	5
and so on	

This is easy to read, but will still be rather long as the maximum number of days absent is 53, and there will be spaces, as there are many numbers of days for which no employee has been absent. To overcome this difficulty it is possible to arrange the days absent in bands. It is necessary to choose a suitable band width, neither so narrow that the table is unduly long, nor so wide that the table is uninformative. In the context of the working week bands of five days seem appropriate:

No. of days' sickness 1.10.x6–31.3.x7

No. of days absent	No. of absentees
1–5	40
6–10	18
11–15	6
16–20	4
21–25	2
26–30	1
31–35	2
36–40	3
41–45	1
46–50	2
51–55	1
Total	80

There does appear to be a high rate of sickness, but in order to draw any conclusions it would be necessary to compare these figures with those for the previous six months, and then to consider what other factors might cause such a high rate of sickness or absenteeism. More information can be added to the table by giving a split between the sexes. There is an equal number of both sexes employed.

No. of days' sickness 1.10.x6–31.3.x7

No. of days absent	No. of absentees		
	Male	Female	Total
1–5	18	22	40
6–10	7	11	18
11–15	4	2	6
16–20	0	4	4
21–25	0	2	2
26–30	1	0	1
31–35	0	2	2
36–40	0	3	3
41–45	1	0	1
46–50	0	2	2
51–55	0	1	1
Totals	31	49	80

This table shows the high rate of women's sickness as compared to the men's. Women generally have a higher rate of days absent for sickness than men, because they are absent for the sickness of their dependants—husbands, children and parents—as well as their own. Even allowing for this fact, their sickness rate does appear to be abnormally high. Again it would be necessary to compare the figures with those of previous six-month periods, and to consider any other factors—which in a small community might include an epidemic of some childhood disease, a teachers' strike, or an exceptionally hard winter—before leaping to any conclusions about the effect of the new chemical on female physiology.

(c)   HINTS ON TABULATION

(i)   Decide on classification and headings.
(ii)   Name the table.
(iii)   Head rows and columns, noting units used.
(iv)   Underline all totals and important results.
(v)   Footnotes should be used to give further details and the source of the data.
(vi)   Neatness and clarity is essential.

2   Pictograms

These present data by means of simple drawings.

Example 3
The population of an area might be represented by stick men, with each man representing 10,000 people.

The population of Maidentop 19x5 (ten thousands)

The advantages of this presentation are that it is extremely simple to understand and makes an immediate visual impact without appearing to be technical. The disadvantages are that it is not accurate to more than half a unit—in the above example to the nearest 5,000 people—and it can be difficult to draw a number of identical symbols. It can also be difficult to make sufficient differentiation between similar symbols, as the following shows:

Example 4

Types of fish caught off the shores of Belmont 19x5 (thousand tonnes)

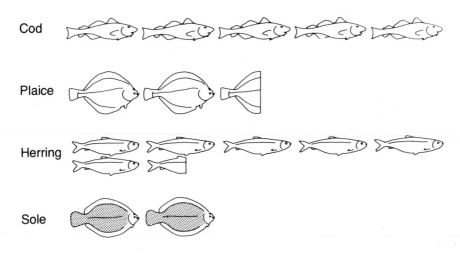

3 Pie Charts

These present data by means of a circular pie divided into sections. They can be used to dramatic effect to show how a sum of money has been spent.

Example 5

Freight Ltd.

Profit and Loss account 31 December 19x3

	£'000
Sales	360
Staff costs	100
Fuel and oil	60
Materials and services	145
Depreciation	20
Operating surplus	35
	360

A circle of a suitable size must be drawn and divided by degrees into the appropriate sections. This is a simple matter as there are 360 degrees in a circle. A base radius is drawn and the angles are measured from it.

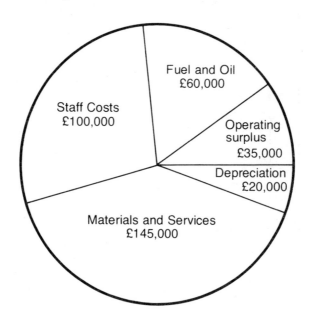

The advantages of this method of presentation are that it is simple to understand and can be used in any situation where an item is divided into sections. It can also be used to compare the situation from year to year. The disadvantages of this method are that it can be difficult to calculate the angles and so is not absolutely accurate. Although it can be used to compare situations from year to year, the circles should have radii proportionate to the size of the total divided. For example:

Sales in 19x3 were £360,000, and were represented by a pie chart with a 4 cm radius; sales in 19x4 were £450,000, a 25% increase, which for purposes of comparison must be represented by a chart with a radius of 5 cm. This can present practical difficulties in construction, with more difficult figures.

4 Bar Charts

These present data by means of horizontal or vertical bars, drawn to scale in order to compare data.

Example 6
Using the information given in Example 4, bar charts can be drawn:

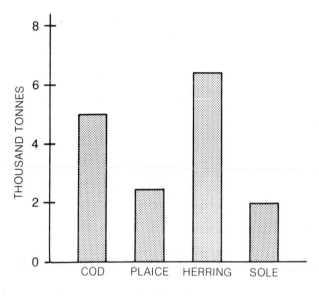

Fig. 21.1

The vertical scale is marked, and horizontal lines help the eye to make comparisons between the relative heights of the bars.

(a)   MULTIPLE BAR CHARTS

Additional information can be included by use of a multiple, or compound bar chart.

Example 7
The fish caught off Belmont during 19x5 and 19x6 can be shown on the same diagram.

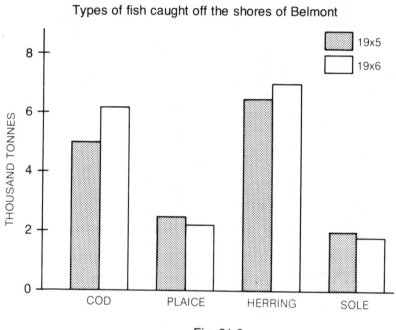

Fig. 21.2

This presentation makes comparison of the annual catch of different fish easy; thus, the drop in the catch of plaice and sole could well be a warning of dwindling stocks. However, if the total catch is under consideration another format is required for easy interpretation.

(b) COMPONENT BAR CHARTS

Example 8
The total catch can be shown on one bar, subdivided into the different varieties of
fish.

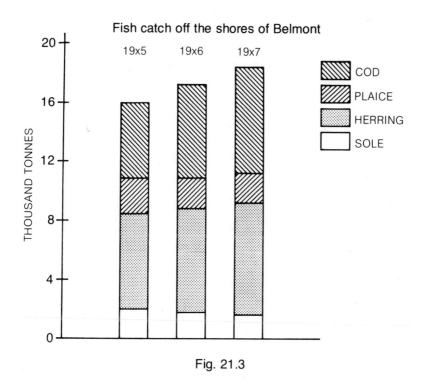

Fig. 21.3

This shows that the overall catch is increasing while the catches of sole and plaice
are decreasing. It is essential that the components appear in the same order in all the
component bar charts, otherwise it would be difficult to make comparisons.

(c)   PERCENTAGE COMPONENT BAR CHARTS

If one wishes to consider the changing proportions of the whole, this can be done by using percentage component bar charts. All the charts are the same length, representing 100%, but the make-up changes.

Example 9

The information given in Figure 21.3 can be re-analysed into percentage component bar charts:

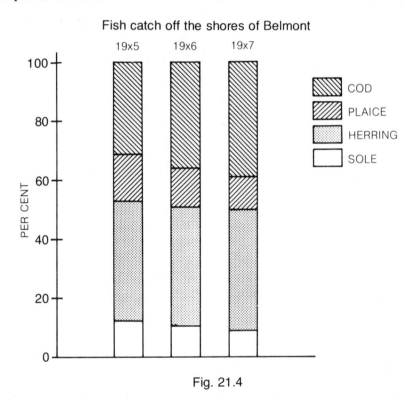

Fig. 21.4

This shows the increasing importance of herring and cod to the total catch, and the diminishing stocks of sole and plaice. The information in this form could easily be shown on a pie chart, which lends itself to showing proportions. The advantages of presenting data by means of bar charts are that they are easy to draw and reasonably accurate. Although comparative quantities are not as easy to understand on a component bar chart as on a pie chart, except where differences are very slight, it is much easier to compare different component bar charts than pie charts. The disadvantage of bar charts is that they look a little more technical than either pictograms or pie charts.

5   Notes on Charts and Diagrams Above

The information shown in Example 4 and in Figs. 21.1 to 21.4 can be presented in tabular form as under. From this it is possible to decide which is the most appropriate presentation for given circumstances, and which is easiest to understand.

Fish catch off the shores of Belmont

Thousand Tonnes

	19X5		19X6		19X7	
	Wght.	%	Wght.	%	Wght.	%
Cod	5·0	31·3	6·2	36·0	7·2	39·1
Plaice	2·5	15·6	2·2	12·8	2·0	10·9
Herring	6·5	40·6	7·0	40·7	7·6	41·3
Sole	2·0	12·5	1·8	10·5	1·6	8·7
Totals	16·0	100·0	17·2	100·0	18·4	100·0

6   Histograms

A histogram shows patterns of frequency and is a diagrammatic form of a frequency tabulation. It must not be confused with a historigram which is a graph of a time series.

Example 10
From the data given in the completed frequency table from Example 2 on page 209, a histogram can be drawn with the horizontal axis scaled in the class intervals of days absent, and the vertical axis in the number of absentees. See Fig. 21.5.

In this form of presentation the mode item is the one with the highest bar. So in the above example the modal number of days' absence lies between 1 and 5.

In a frequency table it is common for the ultimate class interval to be open-ended, for example 'over 35 days', or 'more than £50'. In this situation the final class interval is assumed to be the same size as the others unless there is reason to believe this is not so.

(a)   UNEQUAL CLASS INTERVALS

Certain data falls naturally into unequal class intervals, for instance that relating to workers is often split into '16 but under 21', to include apprentices, then in fairly constant 10-year bands until the age of 50, and this often covers the final fifteen

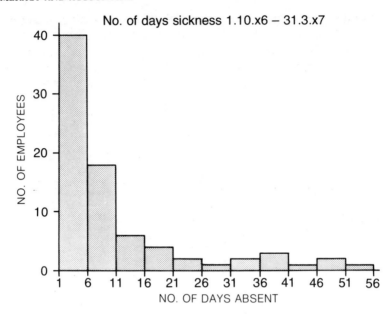

Fig. 21.5

years of working life '50 but under 65', or it can be split into a ten- and a five-year band. In some cases it may be sensible to divide the data into unequal class intervals because the items within a group are not spread evenly throughout it, or because certain classes contain few or no items and it is sensible to combine them to obtain a higher frequency.

Example 11
The age distribution among the hundred workers at the chemical factory was as follows:

Age (years)	No. of employees
16–20	5
21–29	18
30–39	35
40–49	24
50–64	18
Total	100

Obviously, as one is using a standard scale, the bars of the small class intervals will be narrower than those of the large class intervals, proportionate to interval. The band 16–20 covers five years, the interval 21–29 covers 9 years, the two subsequent bands cover ten years and the final band fifteen years. However, the *area* of each bar must be proportional to the class frequencies. That is, if one

218

interval is half the standard interval then the height of the bar must be doubled to compensate for the narrow width. Conversely, if the class interval is double the standard interval, the height of the bar must be halved.

With the above example the standard interval will be taken as ten years. The calculations for the height of the bars are as follows:

$$\frac{\text{Frequency} \times \text{standard interval}}{\text{Actual Interval}}$$

$$16\text{--}20 \quad \frac{5 \times 10}{5} = 10$$

$$21\text{--}29 \quad \frac{18 \times 10}{9} = 20$$

$$50\text{--}64 \quad \frac{18 \times 10}{15} = 12$$

From these figures a histogram may be drawn:

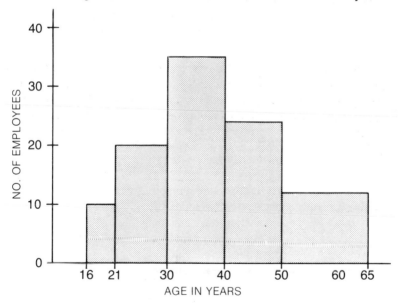

Age distribution of workers in the chemical factory

Fig. 21.6

Theoretically it is possible to reduce class intervals to the ideal limit of the histogram which is a frequency curve. This is an extremely accurate picture of a frequency distribution, and there are various formulae for ascertaining with a high degree of accuracy and with—what is more important—carefully defined degrees of accuracy, the distribution of a whole from a relatively small random sample. This is the basis on which statistical surveys are organised.

For example, the auditors from any large firm of accountants will use random sampling methods to view a minority of the financial transactions undertaken during the year, and from these be able to make a logical decision regarding the sufficiency of the accounting records and the accuracy of the accounts. This has considerable advantages in that it reduces substantially the length and the cost of the statutory audit, and enables the accounts to be published speedily and the office routine to undergo a minimum of disruption.

There are many other business applications: another practical example is that one can test a small sample of the factory's production to ensure that it meets the appropriate specifications as regards strength, safety, weight, size, etc. and be confident within strictly defined degrees that the entire production measures up to this standard.

7 Summary

Diagrams and charts to represent given data can be extremely flexible. There is considerable scope for imaginative work and the use of artistic talent. The main points to bear in mind are that the diagrams must be clearly labelled and headed, and be an appropriate representation both of the data and for the anticipated audience. The use of colour may be appropriate both to differentiate between data and to suggest connections by different shades of the same base colour.

Questions

21.1 Define and differentiate between dependent and independent variables and give an example of the two interacting.

21.2 Differentiate between discrete and continuous variables. State whether the following characteristics are discrete or continuous:
(a) The number of people killed on the roads daily.
(b) The temperature on the Air Ministry roof.
(c) The weight of new-born babies in a London hospital.
(d) The number of students studying accountancy.
(e) The size of a family.

21.3 Into what classes must the following be divided in order that every item will appear in one, and only in one class? The data is under headings of: mineral, opaque, neither mineral nor opaque.

21.4 Construct a frequency table from the following data using class intervals of £10, and draw a histogram.

Weekly earnings for group of workers. Week ending 31.5.19x7. £

16	65	63	54	59	55	22	32	56	55	25	25	18	31	51	59
45	48	17	51	50	53	50	36	41	55	37	61	51	27	38	55
49	43	48	47	39	51	29	46	46	55	36	51	63	49	48	45
18	53	53	45	44	57	58	45	39	55	45	42	49	50	40	41

21.5 From the following data construct a pie chart:

Factory production 19x1
Thousand tonnes

Iron	240
Copper	120
Steel	300
Stainless Steel	60
Total	720

21.6 Construct a multiple bar chart to show the information given in the table below.

X Y Z Company
Sales £'000

	19x1	19x2	19x3
Home	570	600	660
Export	190	300	440
	760	900	1,100

21.7 Construct a percentage component bar chart to represent the information given in the above table.

21.8 Construct a histogram from the following data:

Widgets produced by widget-makers January 19x6

No. of widgets	No. of workers
0—19	20
20—29	110
30—39	250
40—49	80
50—69	40

21.9 Construct a histogram from the following data:

Age of skilled machinists in corsetry factory

Age in years	No. of machinists
16–20	25
21–25	30
26–29	4
30–39	41
40–49	62
50–59	35

Comment on the age-pattern revealed.

Chapter 22 ELEMENTARY LINEAR PROGRAMMING

This book has dealt with arithmetic, which is the basic tool for all mathematical calculation; the conventional methods of recording financial transactions and the systems whereby financial data is collected; and statistics, the science by which data can be tabulated, presented graphically, and used to predict the characteristics of hitherto unknown data. All this information is given for one purpose, to enable business problems to be solved from a well-informed and logical basis. One technical method which can be used to solve certain business problems is known as linear programming.

Statistical methods are concerned with the collection of data and with drawing inferences from it; they do not exercise any control over the data, or by themselves solve problems. It must constantly be remembered that the accuracy of results depends on the accuracy of the original data; as with computers, so with any calculations, 'garbage in, garbage out'. However, linear programming is a mathematical technique which will give the optimum solution to problems where the variables involved are directly proportionate to one another.

Examples of this are: the cost of raw materials and the quantity ordered, unless a quantity discount is given; the raw materials consumed and the volume of production; the time taken to process a batch and the size of the batch.

In practice, these variables may not be strictly directly proportional, but in the majority of cases the results are still valid. It should be noted that, in a business context, the optimum solution will usually maximise profit, although there may be other considerations such as utilising a body of skilled workers and not permitting them to disperse; but this will not necessarily require the full utilisation of resources. The types of problems solved by this technique are those relating to allocation of resources, distribution and transportation. The more difficult problems may require a computer to perform the calculations but the technique itself is basically simple.

1 Allocation of Resources

In many business situations resources have to be allocated between competing products under certain constraints in such a way as to achieve the optimum return. Practical examples of this include:

Product composition   The most economical combination of raw materials that will produce a satisfactory product. With processed food the result must be both nutritious and edible.

Production scheduling   The most efficient use of both machinery and manpower to minimise cost and maximise output. It may be the most effective use of resources to deal with seasonal demand, when the object is to keep production running smoothly and at the same time not incur high storage costs.

The problems can be formulated as equations, and solved mathematically. Simple problems with only two variables can be solved graphically, and this method has the advantage of being easy to follow so the basic principles can be established.

Example 1

A farmer manufactures two types of cheese, an 'ordinary' cheese, and a 'special farm' cheese. After separating the milk the process times for a batch of each kind of cheese are:

| | *Process time (hours)* | |
	'ordinary'	'special farm'
Churning	2	3
Moulding	$2\frac{1}{2}$	2

There are 2100 hours available for each process. There is a limited demand for the more expensive 'special farm' cheese, and only 400 batches can be sold; there is unlimited demand for 'ordinary' cheese. Every batch of 'ordinary' cheese makes a contribution to fixed overheads and profit of £200, while every batch of 'special farm' cheese makes a contribution of £400.

First, this must be formulated as a series of equations, or inequalities as they are called, for they are not true equations.

Let x be the number of batches of 'ordinary' cheese produced.

Let y be the number of batches of 'special farm' cheese produced.

The time taken to churn the batches cannot be longer than 2100 hours.

So $2x + 3y$ must be equal to or less than 2100.

This can be written $\qquad 2x + 3y \leq 2100$

The time taken to mould the cheese cannot be longer than 2100

So $\qquad\qquad 2\frac{1}{2}x + 2y \leq 2100.$

There are many solutions to these equations, but the object is to find the solution which will maximise the contribution. The contribution, C, is equal to £200x + £400y.

In order to draw a graph a suitable scale must be chosen; to arrive at a reasonable scale, consider the maximum values of x and y that should be shown.

Using the first equation, if y equals 0, x equals 1050. This figure should be about half-way along the scale. Using the second equation, if x equals 0, y equals 1050. However, in this case this seems to be the maximum value of y required, as in the solution it cannot be greater than 400.

The equations were chosen as the ones in which x and y had the greatest value.

A graph can now be constructed and the two equations represented as straight lines.

Taking the inequality $2x + 3y \leq 2100$. If y equals 0, x equals 1050; this is one end of the line.

If the converse is true and x equals 0, y equals 700; this is the other end of the line, which can be drawn and labelled.

Taking the inequality $2\frac{1}{2}x + 2y \leq 2100$. If y equals 0, x equals 840.

Conversely, if x equals 0, y equals 1050. The second line can be drawn between these points and labelled. Finally, there is the constraint that y cannot be greater than 400, so a horizontal line must be drawn across the y axis at 400.

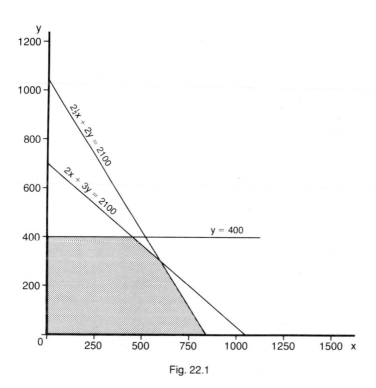

Fig. 22.1

The intersecting lines form a polygon, that is an irregular shape composed of several straight sides, and the solution must lie within it. It is sometimes known as the feasibility polygon.

The object now is to find the single solution to maximise the contribution. This solution will lie at one of the corners of the polygon. A line can be drawn to represent the contribution, C; this will increase the further it moves from nought. $C = £200x + £400y$.

To draw the first line, let the profit be any common multiple of 200 and 400, for instance £120,000.

If the profit is £120,000 and y equals 0, x equals $\dfrac{120,000}{200} = 600$

This is one end of the line.

If the profit is £120,000 and x equals 0, y equals $\dfrac{120,000}{400} = 300$

This is the other end of the line.

The process can be repeated, and a series of parallel lines will be produced; the line that goes through a corner at the furthest point from nought, provides the correct solution. This can be found by moving a ruler until the point is reached and drawing the line.

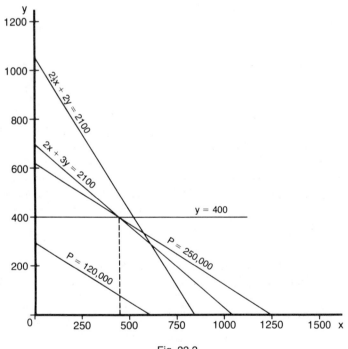

Fig. 22.2

Dotted lines can be drawn from this point to the x and y axes.

The maximum contribution of £250,000 is achieved when 450 batches of 'ordinary' cheese and 400 batches of 'special farm' cheese are produced. As graphical solutions tend to be inaccurate, an arithmetical check should be made.

The contribution of 450 batches of 'ordinary' cheese
is $\qquad 450 \times 200 = £90,000$

The contribution of 400 batches of 'special farm'
cheese is $\qquad 400 \times 400 = £160,000$

Total contribution $\qquad £250,000$

The number of churning hours required are: $(450 \times 2) + (400 \times 3) = 2100$

The number of moulding hours required are: $(450 \times 2\frac{1}{2}) + (400 \times 2) = 1825$.

Both of these are within the specified limits.

The graph shows how an alteration in any of the factors will affect the solution. For example, if the constraint of producing only 400 batches of special farm cheese were changed to 600, then it would be more profitable to produce 600 batches of 'special farm' cheese and only 150 batches of 'ordinary' cheese.

It must be remembered that it is not possible to produce negative quantities, and only positive solutions may be considered.

2   Transportation and Distribution Problems

These problems occur in various situations, for example: A firm has several factories which produce the same goods but at varying costs; demand does not equal the combined capacity of the factories; how then should production be allocated? Or where a business sells its products to different distributors from several factories, how should the goods be allocated in order to minimise transport cost? Or in what way should labour be deployed in order to minimise labour costs?

The linear programming method of problem solving is merely the old-fashioned trial and error method but undertaken in a systematic way, so each solution is tried only once, and the best solution is indicated.

Example 2
Chemicax Ltd. manufacture five different chemicals at three factories. All the factories can produce any of the chemicals, in any combination but at differing costs.

The demand for the chemicals, in tonnes, is:

A	B	C	D	E
50	25	20	30	25

The factory production capacities, in tonnes, are:

I	2	3
30	40	80

The profit in pounds obtained from each tonne of production at the different factories is shown by the following table:

Factory	Chemicals				
	A	B	C	D	E
I	50	40	20	25	30
2	20	15	5	45	20
3	15	30	10	30	20

The table must be reformulated to include both requirements and capacities.

		50	25	20	30	25
		A	B	C	D	E
30	I	50	40	20	25	30
40	2	20	15	5	45	20
80	3	15	30	10	30	20

The first point to note is that supply and demand are equal so all the figures will be required. The aim is to maximise the profit, so the table is considered systematically taking the highest profit first. In this example it is £50 for chemical A produced at factory 1. A quick check shows that production at either of the other factories is much less profitable; the differential of £30 is the greatest to be found on the table, so no other course can be more profitable than to produce 30 tonnes of A at factory 1. So this can be circled and marked with a small 30. 30 tonnes is the entire productive capacity of factory 1, which can be crossed out, and as only a further 20 tonnes of chemical A is required this figure can be substituted for the 50. The table now looks like this:

		~~50~~ 20	25	20	30	25
		A	B	C	D	E
~~30~~	I	(50) 30	40	20	25	30
40	2	20	15	5	45	20
80	3	15	30	10	30	20

The procedure is repeated, the highest profit is now £45 for chemical D produced at factory 2. There is no differential between factories 2 and 3 greater than £15, so 30 tonnes of D, produced at factory 2, represents part of the optimum solution.

The highest remaining profit is £30, for chemical B produced at factory 3; there is no differential between factories 2 and 3 greater than £15, so this represents part of the solution.

The table now looks like this:

	50^{20}	25	20	30	25
	A	B	C	D	E
30 I	$(50)^{30}$	40	20	25	30
40^{10} 2	20	15	5	$(45)^{30}$	20
80^{55} 3	15	$(30)^{25}$	10	30	20

20 tonnes of A, 20 tonnes of C and 25 tonnes of E are required; only factories 2 and 3 have spare capacity. It makes no difference where E is produced, so consideration of this can be left until last. It is £5 cheaper to produce A at factory 2, so 10 tonnes of A will be made there, and factory 3 will make 10 tonnes of A, 20 tonnes of C and 25 tonnes of E.

	50	25	20	30	25
	A	B	C	D	E
30 I	$(50)^{30}$	40	20	25	30
40 2	$(20)^{10}$	15	5	$(45)^{30}$	20
80 3	$(15)^{10}$	$(30)^{25}$	$(10)^{20}$	30	$(20)^{25}$

The final solution shows that the columns of small figures cross cast.

The profit made will be:

Factory 1	30 tonnes of A at £50		£1,500
Factory 2	10 tonnes of A at £20	£200	
	30 tonnes of D at £45	£1,350	£1,550
Factory 3	10 tonnes of A at £15	£150	
	25 tonnes of B at £30	£750	
	20 tonnes of C at £10	£200	
	25 tonnes of E at £20	£500	£1,600
			£4,650

With a small number of figures the optimum solution can often be found immediately by taking note of comparative costs. In more complicated situations it may be necessary to experiment to see if a better solution can be obtained. There may well be more than one solution which gives the same profit. If the problem is framed giving costs or distances which are to be minimised the procedure is the same, but the lowest costs or shortest distances are selected first. When supply and demand are unequal the least profitable combinations can be eliminated.

The methods for solving both allocation and transportation problems can be expressed algebraically, and as such can be solved by the use of a computer. Simple examples can be done mentally, but these methods quickly become tedious when a great number of factors have to be included.

Questions

22.1 Mrs. Hund runs a boarding kennels for beagles and labradors. She can take up to 54 dogs at any one time but only 45 beagles and 30 labradors. A beagle requires 3 hours walking a week, and a labrador 2 hours. There are 3 kennelmaids who can walk dogs for 40 hours each during the week, and a schoolboy who walks dogs for 6 hours on a Saturday.

Draw a graph to show these constraints and shade the feasibility polygon.

If the weekly profit on a beagle is £12, and on a labrador £9, show graphically the point where the profit will be greatest. What is the most profitable combination of dogs?

22.2 A mill near Aberdeen produces tartan cloth in the Forbes colours. Two qualities, standard and heavy duty, are made and they require the following quantities of wool per square metre:

Wool	Standard A	Heavy duty B
Blue	115 g	140 g
White	110 g	40 g
Green	115 g	230 g

The supplies of wool are limited to 1130 kg of blue, 850 kg of white and 1700 kg of green.

Both types of cloth can be woven on the machines at a rate of 10 square metres an hour, and a maximum of 900 machine-hours is available during a month.

Draw a graph to show these constraints and shade the feasibility polygon.

If the profit on a square metre of standard tartan is 75 pence, and on heavy duty tartan is £1, how much of each kind should be produced in order to maximise profit?

Show your solution on the graph.

22.3 David Päpas owns a taxi firm. He has three garages which contain 2, 3, and 2 cars respectively. One wet evening when all the cars are in their garages, 5 phone calls are received. Messrs. A, C and E require one taxi, and Messrs. B and D two taxis each. All require them immediately, if not sooner. The distances of the clients from the garages in miles are tabled below:

Garages	Clients				
	A	B	C	D	E
1	3	9	5	3	3
2	2	5	7	4	1
3	8	3	1	6	9

Which taxis should collect which clients in order to minimise the mileage?

22.4 Four general maintenance workers are available for repairs and maintenance in the company's factories. All the men are highly skilled and can tackle any task; they all work a thirty-five hour week. In one week there are five jobs to be done which will require the following number of hours' work:

Job	A	B	C	D	E
Hours	50	10	20	25	35

The cost per hour in pounds of the men working on the different jobs varies as shown by the following table:

Men	Jobs				
	A	B	C	D	E
1	6	7	5	9	10
2	9	10	11	8	5
3	11	11	13	7	8
4	8	12	15	6	14

Assign the men to the jobs in the most economical manner.

Chapter 23 INTERPRETATION OF ACCOUNTS

1 Definition

To interpret accounts is to bring out their meaning. Accounts are not the sorting of a jumble of figures to the tidy conclusion of a symmetrical balance sheet, but the key to the past and the future of the business.

2 Explanation

In order to look at published accounts some additional vocabulary is required, as this book does not purport to give a comprehensive course in accounts. Further studies will give greater insight into these headings, which are summarily dealt with here.

Then, in order to rationalise the wealth of information and to pinpoint significant data, ratio analysis may be used. However, it must be remembered that the interpretation of accounts is an art, not an exact science, and that there is no substitute for common sense and commercial judgment. The aim is to form an opinion of the true financial position of the business; the numbers are visible to all but skill and judgment are required to assess their relative importance and unveil their significance.

One looks at different aspects of the accounts depending on the motive for looking. Shareholders look at the profits and the expected dividends or capital return, prospective investors have the same ideas; creditors are concerned that their debts will be paid; while bankers and other financial institutions want to ensure that their investment will be well used and that the business will produce profits sufficient to service the interest and repay the capital. Such lenders will also be looking for security in the form of assets, and for sound management.

3 Vocabulary

Share Capital
The equal parts into which a company's capital is divided and which entitle the holder to a share of the profits. A company will want to raise a given amount of capital on its formation but the directors, prudently looking to future requirements, may authorise the raising of a larger sum. This leads to the possibility of several different figures for capital on the balance sheet. These are:

Authorised capital
the total value of shares that the company may issue as stated in the memorandum.

Issued capital
the value of shares issued by the company even if they are not fully paid.

Paid-up capital
the amount actually paid by members to the company for their shares.

There are different classes of share capital including the two mentioned below:

Preference shares
The holders of these shares are entitled to a fixed rate of dividend out of the profits. They receive this in preference to the ordinary shareholders. Sometimes these shares are redeemable and can be repurchased by the company on a given date; this redemption can only be made out of profits or the proceeds of a new issue of shares.

Ordinary shares
There is no fixed rate of dividend on these but the holders are entitled to the surplus profits of the business. The ordinary shareholders take the greatest risk as there may be no profits available for distribution and their investment may prove worthless if the company performs badly or goes into liquidation.

Share premium account
When a company is first formed it will issue its shares at 'par' or at their nominal value. After a period of time the value of the shares may increase; if the company wants to issue further shares it must do so at the current market price. The difference between the nominal value and the amount the company receives for the new issue of shares is known as the share premium. It is an integral part of the capital of the company and may not be distributed to shareholders.

Reserves
A reserve is an allocation or appropriation of profits. Reserves are made for various reasons: to provide additional working capital, a general reserve; to provide for some anticipated loss or liability, a specific reserve; or to allow for a capital profit, a capital reserve. In a limited company, capital reserves may not be distributed as dividends.

Debentures

These are loans made to the company which are usually secured on its assets. Interest is payable on them and a repayment date is normally fixed. Debentures are issued in much the same way as shares, but there is an important difference between them. A shareholder is a member of the company; he owns a small portion if it and, although he may sell his portion to a new owner, he cannot sell it to the company itself. He is entitled to a share of the profits of the company. The debenture holder, on the other hand, has merely lent money to the company; he receives interest on this and in due course his money will be repaid.

A bank, or other financial institution, will frequently insist that its loan to a business is secured by a debenture. This particular form of debenture is very common.

Fictitious Assets

These are not real 'assets' at all, as they have no value, but are debit balances carried forward on the balance sheet. They may represent losses from the profit and loss account, or capital expenditure which has not resulted in the acquisition of property. The important point to note is that they have no real value.

Intangible assets

These are assets which, while being of genuine value to the business, have no concrete form. Examples of this are patents and copyrights.

Goodwill

There is some debate as to whether this is a fictitious or an intangible asset. Goodwill is the term given to the difference between the valuation of the net assets and the price actually paid when an existing business is purchased. It is argued that one pays more than the valuation of the assets, as one is buying not a heap of artefacts but a flourishing business with existing customers and an established name. If this is so, then the asset is real if intangible. On the other side it is argued that goodwill is just a mechanical device to ensure that the books balance; if this is so, the asset is fictitious. In any event, goodwill must be written off over a number of years; it cannot be said to reflect the popularity of a business at any moment other than the point of sale.

Contingent liability

This is a potential liability which may or may not materialise. It is usually very difficult to quantify. An example would occur if a construction company had erected buildings in which it is feared, but not certainly known, that there may be some structural defect. If this defect materialises the company will be liable, but even if it does materialise it is not known how many buildings will be affected or how severely they may be damaged. It is important to realise that such potential liabilities may threaten the very existence of a business.

Liquidity

The term means that assets are readily convertible into cash. Cash itself is the most

234

liquid asset, followed by bills of exchange and marketable securities. Balance sheets are usually arranged either in the order of least liquidity, with the most stable assets first, from fixed assets down to cash as shown in this book; or in the opposite manner, the order of greatest liquidity, giving pride of place to the cash and going down to the established property.

4 Ratio Analysis

Any figure on the balance sheet may be compared with any other, but for the purpose of understanding the accounts certain comparisons are more important than others.

To illustrate the use of the analysis, consider the accounts of Neutron and Quasar, dealers in spaceships, for two consecutive years (shown overleaf).

GROSS PROFIT PERCENTAGE

This is the ratio of gross profit to turnover, or sales. It gives a guide not only to the profitability of the business but also to the accuracy of the accounts, as the ratio should remain fairly constant from year to year in the absence of special factors.

In Neutron and Quasar the results are:

$$19\text{X}1 \quad \frac{90,000 \times 100}{200,000} = 45\%$$

$$19\text{X}2 \quad \frac{140,000 \times 100}{320,000} = 43.75\%$$

There has been a drop of 1.25% in 19x2. This may be due to any or a combination of the following reasons.

(a)   A change in sales policy. The selling price may have been reduced in order to increase the volume of sales, and in the example sales have increased by 60%, and so increased the net profit.

(b)   Increased costs of materials which have not been passed on to the customer, either because of the sales policy noted above or because of government restrictions.

(c)   A change in the method of stock valuation, which gives a lower valuation than previously. For example, a change from the FIFO method to the LIFO method will usually cause a reduction in the valuation of stock, and hence a reduction in the gross profit percentage.

(a)   An error in the stock count or the stock valuation. This may be detected by a careful analysis of the stock changes between the two years, and inquiry into significant differences.

(e)   An accounting error in that invoices may have been included in purchases and creditors at the year-end but the goods to which they refer are omitted from the stock count. It is of vital importance that the cut-off at the year-end is closely

Neutron and Quasar

Trading and Profit and Loss Account for the year ended 31 December

	19X1 £	19X1 £	19X2 £	19X2 £
Sales		200,000		320,000
Opening stock	30,000		40,000	
Purchases	120,000		195,000	
	150,000		235,000	
Less closing stock	(40,000)		(55,000)	
Cost of sales		110,000		180,000
Gross profit		90,000		140,000
Selling expenses	23,750		36,250	
Administration expenses	20,000		30,000	
Interest	3,750		3,750	
		47,500		70,000
Net Profit		£42,500		£70,000

Balance Sheet

as at December 31

	19X1 Cost £	19X1 Dep. £	19X1 NBV £	19X2 Cost £	19X2 Dep. £	19X2 NBV £
Fixed assets	100,000	20,000	80,000	140,000	25,000	115,000
Current assets						
Stock	40,000			55,000		
Debtors	25,000			35,000		
Cash	8,000			—		
		73,000			90,000	
Less current liabilities						
Creditors	30,500			50,000		
Bank overdraft	—			14,000		
		30,500			64,000	
Net working capital			42,500			26,000
Net value of assets			£122,500			£141,000
Capital						
Opening balance			83,000			97,500
Add profit			42,500			70,000
Less drawings			(28,000)			(51,500)
			97,500			116,000
Long-term loan			25,000			25,000
Capital employed			£122,500			£141,000

controlled. The opposite mistake, including goods in stock but not in creditors, will lead to an overstatement of profit.

(f) Theft. Stock may have been stolen by employees or others, or cash may have been stolen from the till and cash sales understated. It is important to determine the change in gross profit percentage as, if it is not due to causes (a) to (e) above, then the difference has been stolen. From the example, the expected percentage was 45 % and so the loss was 1·25 % of £32,000, which equals £4,000.

A rise in the gross profit percentage could be due to:
(a) An increase in selling price.
(b) A change or error in the stock valuation or stock count leading to an overstatement of the stock.
(c) An error in the cut-off at year-end, so that goods are included in stock but not in creditors.

NET PROFIT PERCENTAGE

This is the ratio of net profit to turnover and shows the proportion of sales revenue which is due to the proprietors, although they are unlikely to withdraw it all.
    The results from the example are:

19X1 $$\frac{42,500 \times 100}{200,000} = 21 \cdot 25 \%$$

19X2 $$\frac{70,000 \times 100}{320,000} = 21 \cdot 87 \%$$

Despite the decrease in the gross profit percentage there has been a small increase in the net profit percentage. This may show the success of a policy of reducing selling prices, as overheads have not increased in proportion to sales.

EXPENSE RATIOS

Study of these shows the proportion of profit consumed by overheads and may be of use in formulating policy. Expenses can be divided into three main groups: fixed, variable and semi-variable. Fixed expenses do not alter with the volume of business; an example of these are rent and rates on premises or, from the illustration, the fixed interest charge on the loan. Variable expenses vary with the volume of business, for example, salesman's commission is directly related to sales. Semi-variable expenses fall between the others; they do vary but not in direct relation to the volume of business. For example, if an increase in turnover is due to an increase in selling prices, the administrative overheads will remain constant, as the same number of invoices will be required but for higher amounts. On the other hand, if the increase in turnover is due to an increase in the volume of sales, then the administration expenses would be expected to increase.

	19X1		19X2	
	£	%	£	%
Selling expenses	23,750	11·87	36,250	11·33
Administration expenses	20,000	10·00	30,000	9·38
Interest	3,750	1·88	3,750	1·17
Net profit	42,500	21·25	70,000	21·87
Gross profit	90,000	45·00	140,000	43·75
Sales	200,000	100·00	320,000	100·00

It can be seen that there has been a slight decrease in all of the costs, which is a satisfactory situation. Any percentage rise in the costs must be carefully investigated with an aim to minimising it.

THE RATE OF TURNOVER OF STOCK

The purpose of establishing this is to keep a check on stock levels and to determine whether they are reasonable for the business. The rate of turnover will vary considerably from business to business. The manufacturer of specialised components may require high stock levels and a low rate of turnover, while the retailer of fresh foods will require low stock levels and a high rate of turnover. The art, as usual, is to achieve the optimum level for the business concerned.

A rough guide to the rate of turnover is obtained by the following formula:

$$\frac{\text{Cost of sales}}{\frac{1}{2}\,(\text{opening stock} + \text{closing stock})}$$

This is only a rough guide, as the stock levels at the year-end may not be indicative of stock levels throughout the year. For example, toy manufacturers build up their stock levels in the summer in readiness for the pre-Christmas rush; while, in temperate climates, manufacturers of garden furniture and equipment re-stock in the winter ready for the spring boom. Many businesses reduce the stock levels at the year-end or choose to end their financial year in a period of low commercial activity, to facilitate stocktaking. To decide a policy on stock levels, these should be looked at on a monthly or even a weekly basis.

Nevertheless, for our intrepid dealers in spaceships their rate of turnover in stock is:

$$19\text{X}1 \qquad \frac{110,000}{\frac{1}{2}\,(30,000 + 40,000)} = 3\cdot14$$

$$19\text{X}2 \qquad \frac{180,000}{\frac{1}{2}\,(40,000 + 55,000)} = 3\cdot79$$

The optimum stock level will keep stock as low as possible while being able to supply customers' requirements. Keeping stock is expensive and requires working

INTERPRETATION OF ACCOUNTS

capital, while if insufficient stocks are available valuable custom may be lost. Without further information it is impossible to comment on the adequacy or otherwise of Quasar and Neutron's stock levels.

RETURN ON CAPITAL EMPLOYED

This is probably the single most important percentage as it tells a proprietor whether he should be in business at all. There is always an element of risk involved in any business and, if it is possible to obtain an equal or greater return on the money markets in risk-free investment, it would seem sensible to do so. In real life the equation is not so simple, as the money markets are volatile, while a business takes some time to build up and may also experience peaks and troughs, not necessarily simultaneous with those in the money market. In addition, a man may prefer to work for himself rather than for a third party. A rough computation may be obtained by using the capital employed at the year-end; a more accurate calculation would use the weighted average for the year.

For Quasar and Neutron the results are:

$$19X1 \quad \frac{42,500 \times 100}{122,500} \quad = 34 \cdot 7\%$$

$$19X2 \quad \frac{70,000 \times 100}{141,000} \quad = 49 \cdot 6\%$$

These results are most satisfactory, showing a considerable increase in profit without commensurate increase in capital employed.

RATIO OF PROPRIETOR'S FUNDS TO OTHER CREDITORS

The proprietor stands to benefit most from the business, so he should take the greatest risk: moreover, if other creditors are bearing a considerable proportion of the risk of a business, the situation will be unstable as in adverse conditions they may be in a position to put the business into liquidation.

It is inaccurate to generalise about ideal ratios, but the owners of a business should always bear at least 50% of the risk, and normally considerably more.

The formula is:

$$\frac{\text{Proprietor's funds}}{\text{Total liabilities}}$$

From the example the results are:

$$19X1 \quad \frac{97,500 \times 100}{97,500 + 30,500 + 25,000} = 63 \cdot 72\%$$

$$19X2 \quad \frac{116,000 \times 100}{116,000 + 64,000 + 25,000} = 56 \cdot 58\%$$

The percentage is on the low side for the business and appears to be worsening. If the business is to continue to expand then it must raise additional capital, either from partners or as a limited company from shareholders. The increase in turnover has led to an increase in creditors and bank overdraft; if this syndrome continues unchecked, the business may find itself in financial difficulties. Overtrading is a common cause of the failure of new businesses.

'GEARING'

This relates to the previous ratio. The capital employed of a business is said to be 'high-geared' when the amount of prior-charge capital in the form of preference shares, debentures or loans is excessive in relation to the owner's or ordinary shareholders' capital. If this happens, a business becomes vulnerable to slight fluctuations in profitability and may find itself overtrading.

From the example, there is a loan with a prior claim on £3,750 of profits. This is immaterial with profits before interest of £46,250 and £73,750. However, if a company had share capital which consisted of £10,000 of ordinary shares and £100,000 of 10% preference shares, the first £10,000 of profit would go to the preference shareholders. If the profits were £12,000 it would be possible to pay a dividend of 20% to the ordinary shareholders. However, if the profits fell by only 16% to £10,000 there would be nothing available for the ordinary shareholders.

SOLVENCY RATIOS

(a) *The current ratio* This is the ratio of current assets to current liabilities. It shows the short-term stability of a business in that current liabilities must be paid out of current assets. Again there is no ideal ratio: it should probably be less than 2:1 and greater than 1:1. In the former case insufficient use is being made of creditors as a source of short-term funds, in the latter the business runs the risk of being unable to pay its creditors. However, businesses vary enormously, and it is the trend in any one business which is significant.

The ratios provided by the example are:

19X1 $\dfrac{73,000}{30,500} = 2\cdot39:1$

19X2 $\dfrac{90,000}{64,000} = 1\cdot4:1$

(b) *The liquidity or acid test ratio* It has yet a third name, the quick asset ratio. It is the comparison of cash and quickly realisable assets to current liabilities, and it shows what immediate cover a business has should all its creditors demand payment. Terminology also varies, and the equation may include debtors, or debtors and prepayments. If the ratio is as high as 1:1 resources are probably lying idle, and many concerns look for a ratio around ·5:1.

From the example again the figures are:

$$19X1 \quad \frac{8{,}000 + 25{,}000}{30{,}500} = 1 \cdot 03 : 1$$

$$19X2 \quad \frac{35{,}000}{64{,}000} = \cdot 55 : 1$$

The ratio is rather volatile, being halved over the year, and requires close scrutiny to ensure that the position does not worsen. As has been mentioned previously, an increase of proprietor's capital would resolve the matter.

5   Criticism of the accounts

A good deal of information can be obtained from published accounts by study of the profit and loss account, balance sheet, statement of the source and application funds and the appended notes. All factors must be considered. Are any loans or other creditors secured on the assets of the business? What is the basis for the valuation of stock? Is the provision for bad debts reasonable, taking the type of business into consideration? Is there an amount on the balance sheet for goodwill? If so, this must be disregarded as it has no value except in a business which is a going concern. Are there any contingent liabilities?

It is important to note whether there has been a change in accounting policy during the year, as this can make a considerable difference to the accounts.

It may also be of use to bear in mind the most common reasons for the failures of companies. Contrary to popular belief, these are not acts of God, vindictive chancellors, or sadistic bank managers, but simple, almost classical, errors of judgment. There is overtrading, a fault with new and often successful companies. Then there is the established family company which has been drained of both financial resources and management expertise, and eventually just runs out of steam, to the amazement of owners and employees alike. Finally, there is the business which has overcommitted itself on just one contract: if something goes wrong with it, there are insufficient resources to fall back on. Here are the pitfalls to avoid, and the signs for which to look.

6   Limitations of Accounts

Certain aspects of a business are not revealed in the accounts, yet may determine its success. In a limited company, information may be gleaned from the directors' report, but otherwise one relies on local sources.

The calibre of management is fundamental to the success of any concern. In a large business a single individual may prove unimportant, but in a small one he can be vital. A business may suffer if a key figure suffers from ill-health or is due to retire.

The workforce is equally important; the business will prosper if they are a homogeneous force enjoying their work and good industrial relations, and suffer if they are not. Finally, there is the aspect of social accounting. One company may obey the letter of the law to the barest minimum, or even openly flout the law incurring only minor fines, in such fields as pollution control or safety regulations. An identical firm may care for the community in which it lives and give money and attention to these matters. The former company may cut costs but to the detriment of the community. As yet, this will not show on any balance sheet, but must be a factor in determining the value of a concern.

Questions

23.1 Ayub Khan wants to open a small general stores. He has capital of £15,000 and proposes to rent premises at £1,500 per annum. His capital is at present invested and brings in an income of £1,800. He is employed as the manager of a store earning £3,000 a year, and his wife earns £1,000 in part-time employment.

The average mark-up of the goods he is selling is 40% of selling price, and the general expenses of the business would be about £1,000 a year.

(a) Prepare a statement to show the lowest amount of turnover which will enable Mr. Khan to receive an income equivalent to his present one.

(b) The premises will hold stock to the value of £4,150. What rate of turnover of stock does Mr. Khan require?

(c) The shop was opened on 1 September 19x3 with stock worth £4,150. This was replaced as soon as possible after a sale. The original estimates proved accurate and sales during the first two months of trading were £3,125. Draft a trading and profit and loss account for the two months ended 31 October, and a balance sheet at that date.

(d) Comment on the first two months of trading.

23.2 Three brothers, Major, Minor and Minimus, received a portion of their parents' estate and each went into business on his own account. Some figures from the first year's trading are given below. All sales were for cash.

	M_1 £	M_2 £	M_3 £
Capital	80,000	70,000	60,000
Fixed assets	50,000	40,000	40,000
Sales	160,000	140,000	100,000
Gross profit	32,000	28,000	20,000
Average stock	24,000	24,000	20,000
Net profit	14,000	12,000	10,000
Creditors	1,800	1,400	1,000

(a)   Calculate for each business:
   (i)   The gross profit percentage.
   (ii)   The net profit percentage.
   (iii)   The rate of turnover of stock.
   (iv)   The return on capital employed.
   (v)   The working capital.
   (vi)   The cash balances.
(b)   Comment on the comparative efficiency of the administration of the businesses, and state which brother you think has the greatest business sense, giving reasons for your opinion.

23.3   The twins Annabelle and Barry, having both inherited money from distant relations, decided to open rival shops. Barry believed he had considerable business acumen: he also had more than twice as much capital as his sister. Annabelle challenged Barry that her business would prove more successful than his, and they agreed to present their figures to an impartial accountant after the first year's trading and to let him judge between them.

	A £	B £
Capital	30,000	67,500
Turnover	225,000	480,000
Gross profit	45,000	120,000
Net profit	22,500	45,000
Average stock	7,500	12,000

(a)   For each business calculate:
   (i)   The gross profit percentage.
   (ii)   The net profit percentage.
   (iii)   The rate of turnover of stock.
   (iv)   The expenses percentage.
   (v)   The return on capital employed.
(b)   As the impartial accountant, compare the results of the two businesses and give your opinion as to which is managed more efficiently.

23.4   The balance sheets of Jonas for two consecutive years are shown below:

	19X1 £	19X2 £		19X1 £	19X2 £
Capital	75,000	75,000	Fixed assets	50,000	49,000
Creditors	5,050	7,900	Stock	8,500	11,500
			Debtors	11,550	14,400
			Cash	10,000	8,000
	80,050	82,900		80,050	82,900

During the year ended 31 December 19x2 sales were £425,000 and the gross profit was £170,000.
(a) Show the working capital for both years.
(b) What was the capital employed in the business on 31 December 19x2?
(c) £4,000 of fixed assets were purchased in 19x2: what was the charge for depreciation in that year?
(d) Calculate the value of purchases in 19x2.
(e) Find the rate of turnover of stock for 19x2.
(f) What conclusions can be drawn from the fact that the capital remains unchanged?

23.5 S. Claus is a manufacturer of toys. He has been having labour problems and, faced with a final demand from the union of goblins, wants to instal machinery. The cost of installing and maintaining this will be the same as his present labour costs. He will be able to increase his output and believes that he can increase sales by lowering his prices. He started to produce the following table, but now seeks your advice:

Units sold	Cost of sales	Turnover	Gross profit	Expenses	Net profit	Return on capital
25,000	24,000	37,000	13,000	3,000	10,000	10%
30,000	28,000	45,000		4,000		
35,000	32,000	53,000		5,000		
40,000	36,000	60,000		6,000		
45,000	40,000	64,000		7,000		
50,000	43,000	68,000		8,000		

You extract from him the fact that his present capital is £100,000 and his last trading and profit and loss account follows:

Sales		37,000
Cost of sales	24,000	
Expenses	3,000	
Net profit	10,000	
	£37,000	£37,000

(a) Advise Santa of the level of output he should aim at.
(b) Further discussions reveal that the new machine can only produce 35,000 units a year, and another machine would cost £10,000. There would be no additional maintenance costs, but the money would be borrowed at an interest rate of 20%.
(c) Advise Santa, taking the new information into account.

23.6 Bella Street purchased a business for £80,000 and started trading on April Fool's day 19x5. From the following information prepare a trading and profit and loss account for her first year of trading, and a balance sheet as at 31 March 19x6. Give as much detail as possible.

At 31 March 19x6:

Fixed assets	75,000
Net working capital	40,000
Long-term loan	25,000
Drawings	7,500
Current ratio	2:1
Liquidity Ratio	1:1
Net profit percentage	20%
Gross profit percentage	30%

The cash balances total one-third of the value of debtors.

INDEX